"Want to go head-to-head, one-on-one with the Almighty? Tole Lege! Pick up this book and read. You may be sure that God has never lost an argument. So don't expect to shove any anti-God viewpoint into his worldview. But God is a good listener, and throughout this book he visits with Robert Don Hughes, who having gained his ear asks him all those tough questions you've always wanted to have answered. God gets a bit colloquial in this book, but he never surrenders his integrity. A good read. A great idea!"

Dr. Calvin Miller, professor, Beeson Divinity School

"After the New Testament, Christians started to think questions were a sign of doubt. In the New Testament, questions were welcomed and answered by Jesus. In that same spirit, Bob Hughes asks and answers the tough questions. Rather than answering with the typical cultural answers, the author goes to the source for the right answers. God is not afraid of the tough questions; he provides the answers in his Word. This book answers the questions people are asking today by mining the answers provided in God's Word written long ago."

Rev. Ed Stetzer, strategic networks manager,
North American Mission Board

"In the Bible we discover God's portrait of himself. In a creative and engaging manner, Robert Hughes explores the significance, impact, and comfort believers can experience when they come face to face with the true and living God. You will enjoy this book. You will be encouraged as well."

Daniel L. Akin, president,
Southeastern Baptist Theological Seminary

QUESTIONING GOD

Honest Answers
to Tough Questions

Robert Don Hughes

BakerBooks

Grand Rapids, Michigan

Published by Baker Books
a division of Baker Publishing Group
P.O. Box 6287, Grand Rapids, MI 49516-6287
www.bakerbooks.com

Printed in the United States of America

Library of Congress Cataloging-in-Publication Data
Hughes, Robert Don, 1949–
    Questioning God : honest answers to tough questions / Robert Don
    Hughes.
        p.   cm.
    ISBN 0-8010-6493-7 (pbk.)
    1. God. 2. Imaginary conversations. I. Title.
BT103.H84 2005
231—dc22   2004022336

This book is for
Leigh Conver and Ed Stetzer
Gerald Roe and Al Jackson
Danny Akin and Mark Terry
Malcom Hester and Bill Whittaker

They carried me, but not as pallbearers.
Instead, they tore up the roof and let me
down on ropes.

CONTENTS

Introduction

I wish I could hear God's voice. I mean audibly, you know? When it's clearly God speaking and not just the "still, small voice" of a mental impression. That may or may not be God speaking. Oh, there have been a number of times in my life when I have felt that "clear impression" of the direction of the Holy Spirit. But that isn't quite the same, is it? Not like hearing God speak audibly, or seeing an angel, or having a finger write legible words on a wall.

My father died about ten years ago. At times I would really like to talk to him now—to ask him specific questions, to hear his wisdom again. Of course, if I close my eyes and think his face into my mind, I can talk to him. And because I knew him so well and generally knew what his reactions would be whenever I spoke to him during his lifetime, I think I can probably guess what he would say. If I wanted to, I could write whole dialogues with my father and probably come pretty close to what an actual conversation with him would be like.

I did the same thing with the person of Satan years ago while writing a book called *Satan's Whispers*. Although the book was well received, writing it was generally a terrible experience. I had set out to write a series of dialogues dealing with the most frequent lies Satan tells us, and as I began to write each morning, I opened a dialogue with the evil one, which left me drained and depressed. When Calvin Miller reviewed the book, he gave it a nine out of ten—one point off because he found it unsettling that a Christian writer should know the devil so well. Since that time I've had many other conversations with that evil presence. I shudder to admit I still hear that voice so clearly. Not an audible voice, of course, just a "mental impression" of what the evil one might say to me in conversation. Too often I have listened.

"Wouldn't it be a whole lot better to carry on such a conversation with the Lord?" I asked myself. "Wouldn't it be a blessing to others to describe such conversations—conversations much like those I know other Christians carry on with God as they walk daily with him?" I was impressed with the WWJD strategy—the spiritual strategy of asking oneself, "What would Jesus do?" in this situation or that. Essentially it's like entering into dialogue with God—in a sense asking him, "How should I react to this problem?" and listening for his response. That's all this book seeks to do—open up conversations with God so we may hear his comforting words.

Much as Satan seeks to distract and confuse us in his quest to steal, devour, and destroy the blessings God seeks to bestow on us, God regularly speaks to us. Not audibly, no—at least, that hasn't been my experience. But if we let the Holy Spirit train us to listen, we can hear that still, small voice rising above the lies and distortions the evil one seeks to place in our minds. The purpose of this book is to help us all—myself included—hear God's voice more clearly. Much as I could carry on a mental dialogue with my departed earthly father because I knew him so well, the Christian can carry on a mental dialogue with our heavenly Father and grow to know him better.

Questioning God seeks to carry on a running conversation with God. I do not claim any inspiration for the words I put into his mouth. These are my imaginary conversations with my heavenly Father, but I think I know him well enough to know what he would say. Which brings up an important thought: how can we know God?

I've studied theology. I have a Ph.D. in the field, actually, and have taught for years in colleges and seminaries. Does that qualify me to talk about how to hear and know God's voice? Not necessarily. It helps, of course. I've read many of those heavy theological tomes that talk about the nature of God, the person of God, the names of God, the purposes of God, and so on. I've learned the names of high-sounding theological categories such as Christology, soteriology, ecclesiology, and eschatology. But one of the main things I've learned in reading theologians is that they tend to write for other theologians. They write in a specialized language only theologians can understand. I've just given you some examples. (In fact, I noticed that some of the words I listed above aren't even in my spell-checker.) New seminary students often have trouble shifting gears from the common questions they are asked in Sunday school to the questions phrased by theologians. They're the same questions, really, but theologians tend to use many more very large words to seek to answer them. This can lead to a potentially tragic outcome. I'm afraid that when some seminary students graduate, they are less able to answer common-variety questions about God than when they started their theological studies. I don't think that's wise. I don't think that's helpful. I don't think that's what God intends!

I think God intends for us to talk to him at any time, from any place, and to begin to know what he would say. But how can we come to understand God? He is, after all, sovereign and transcendent (to use more theological jargon that sometimes obscures God more than it reveals him). Honestly, I think that's exactly why "the Word became flesh and dwelt among us" (John 1:14). I think that's exactly why God lived among people in human form in the person of Christ Jesus. It's a communication problem, really, and God solved it in the best possible way: when his people (the Jews) demonstrated clearly that they either couldn't understand him or wouldn't understand him when he spoke through the Law and the Prophets, he made a personal visit. He spoke to all people in all times through a living, human presence people could clearly understand. The writer of Hebrews makes this clear at the beginning of that wonderful book: "God, who in different ways and various approaches talked to our fathers in the past through the prophets, has recently talked to us through his Son . . . through whom he also made the world" (1:1–2, author's paraphrase). The basic point of this verse is that God wants to speak to us. He wants to make himself known to us as clearly as possible. In fact, the basic principle of Scripture is that God seeks to be in relationship with his creation—all of it.

After all, how can we understand what we've never experienced? Have you ever tried to explain a complicated reality to a child? If you're not careful, you can end up confusing more than clarifying, especially if you use technical language the child doesn't have the experience to understand. If we really want to explain things clearly to a child, we look for terms and events he or she can readily recognize and respond to. This is called "illustration," and all the best preachers are really good at it. Jesus was the best of all—he used parables to explain the kingdom of God. While some might argue that the parables were used to veil the truth to all but the disciples, I think the evidence proves exactly the opposite. The people listened to Jesus because he made the truth of God understandable to them through illustration.

I learned this lesson best while serving as a missionary in Africa. I quickly found that all my theological jargon was useless—not useless to me, for I understood it, but useless to my audience. They needed simple, clear illustrations drawn from their own experience that could help them understand God better. Since that time I have pleaded with my students to find illustrations that illustrate rather than obfuscate, or "hide" or "confuse" or "bewilder." "Why would God want to bewilder those whom he loves and seeks to have fellowship with?" I ask myself. My answer—which I believe is from God—is, he doesn't. From the beginning he has sought ways to reveal himself to us, and he still seeks to do that—through his Word, through the Holy Spirit, and through the body of Christ.

And he has found many different ways to do this. God is an excellent communicator; we just don't always listen. My sister used to have a dog named Spreckles (after a brand of sugar—he was snow white). Spreckles was deaf. Her owners had to communicate with her through hand signals, which she clearly understood. When she didn't want to do what they were telling her to do, she'd learned to just look away. Sometimes we don't hear God because we are looking away. We don't intend to hear him. That can't be you; you're reading this book.

Sometimes we don't hear God because of the many other competing voices in our heads. I've already said that the evil one speaks regularly to me. Now, the devil is an expert in obfuscation! Then there are all those other voices that compete for our attention through the media. One communication scholar researching messages in the 1970s suggested this: because of radio, television, and more frequent interaction with other people in a crowded urban environment, he heard twenty times as many messages per day as his grandfather did in the 1920s. I wonder how many more messages we are assaulted with each day in the twenty-first century? It is difficult, sometimes, to "tune in" the voice of God. Maybe this book can help.

Sometimes we don't hear God because we don't know him well enough to recognize his voice. I think that's becoming more of a problem in our postmodern society. People today know less and less about God, or they have heard such a steady stream of conflicting messages about God that they wouldn't know his "still, small voice" if they were to hear it. That's part of the focus of this book. We need to "draw near to God" so he can draw near to us. That's the promise of James 4:8—God wants to do just that. But how, exactly, do we draw near to him? How do we hear God's comforting voice?

One way, of course, is by reading his Word. That's why a major part of each of the following chapters is a listing of Scripture references. But Scripture is not necessarily self-explanatory, or it wouldn't need to be explained from the pulpit through preaching. Scripture is our basic point of reference—the only thing we can be certain that God has said to us. But through studying Scripture and listening to the Holy Spirit to "grow in the grace and knowledge of our Lord and Savior Jesus Christ" (2 Pet. 3:18), we can come to the place where we can know what our heavenly Father would say to us if we could carry on a dialogue with him—just as I can imagine a conversation with my departed dad.

Which brings me to one of the really good things I learned in a seminary philosophy class. It was a doctoral seminar on religious language—and most of what we read was as thick as potato soup. There was this argument, you see, back at the beginning of the twentieth century, about "God talk." The debate was about whether it was even possible to talk about God at all, since nothing about God could be proven scientifically. Christian philosophers weighed in with various arguments, some easily understandable, some less so—and then I read I. T. Ramsey, which illustrated something for me in a powerful way.*
Ramsey said that the only way we can talk about God is in terms of what we can humanly understand. That is limited, of course, but necessary. We certainly cannot talk about God in terms we don't understand, right? It's like trying to explain complicated things to children without using illustrations. Ramsey called these explanations "models," and I've used one constantly throughout this introduction—the father model. I was blessed to have a father who loved God and served God and sought to be like God in his thinking and speaking. Not everyone is so

*Ian T. Ramsey, *Models and Mystery* (London: Oxford University Press, 1964).

15

blessed, so this model is a problem for some. But I clearly understood when Ramsey said that the father model is one of the primary human terms for understanding God. This is so, however, only when an infinite qualifier is added. The infinite qualifier we most often use when speaking of the father is another phrase I've used several times already—our *heavenly* Father.

Ramsey's point was this: we can take a human term such as *father*, which we easily understand, and modify it with a word such as *heavenly*, which we can only imagine—and still get a pretty good picture of God. Good enough for this present life, in any case. Life itself is another model. When we add the infinite qualifier *eternal* to it, we can understand enough about what heaven is like to live our earthly lives hoping for it. *Everlasting* is another good infinite qualifier for both father and life. *Holy* is a qualifier that can be applied to Scripture, or to God himself, or to most anything we relate to God. It means "separate, set apart, beyond." When we use it to refer to God or his Word, we acknowledge that these things fit in a category that is beyond us—that we need to examine with humility and reverence.

Ramsey suggested that these qualifiers help us take a common, easily understandable word and mentally throw it into infinity—thereby understanding more about God and drawing closer to him. That's what this book is about—models of God, drawn from Scripture, amplified into infinity in order to help us know him better. These are not models of God that I've made up; God has used them of himself in his *holy* Book! And he has used them, I believe, for one primary purpose: to help us draw comfort from him. These are not cold, technical terms for God drawn from classical theology textbooks but warm images of our God's loving embrace—God's comforts. Do you know these comforting concepts?

Let me make a suggestion for how to read this book. Each chapter begins with a question I hear people asking about God. These may be very familiar questions to you. Look down the table of contents and find the question you find yourself asking God most frequently. Then read the dialogue, the Scripture, and the suggestions for prayer provided in that chapter. My prayer is that *Questioning God* will help you hear God's voice speaking to *you*.

1

"Does God Really Hear My Prayers?"

Our heavenly Father, we thank thee for—"

"You're welcome," God interrupts.

I stop, stunned. "You . . . you spoke to me!" I gasp, blinking in shock.

"Yes," God responds calmly. "Didn't you speak to me first?"

"Well . . . yeah, but . . ."

"But what?"

"But . . . but I didn't expect you to answer me!"

"What's the point of prayer if you don't expect me to answer?" God asks.

"I . . . it's . . . just that I'm not used to you actually responding to my prayers!"

"Is that it?" God asks. "Or is it that you just don't listen for my response?"

"I'm not accustomed to hearing voices in my head," I say, a bit defensively, I suppose.

"And you're really not doing that *now*," God answers—accurately, of course. "Let's be clear about this. You're writing. You're listening to me with your imagination—writing what you think I would say if I were to respond audibly to you. And you're also very aware of that person who is 'listening' to us both—the reader. But that doesn't mean you're not really hearing me. In fact, I think you are listening to me quite carefully at the moment. And I like that, because you usually don't."

"I . . . I what?" I choke. "Now, wait—"

"If you're going to write this, be honest with yourself. I'm certainly going to be honest with you. And here's the problem. Much of the time you don't really listen to me at all. Most people don't when they pray. They just talk *at* me. They tell me all their problems, give me their wish lists as if I'm some celestial Santa Claus, then go on their way without waiting to hear my response to them."

"Uh, maybe that's because . . . most of us don't know how to listen to you?" I suggest.

"You do," he tells me. When I fake astonishment and false humility at this, he adds, "I'm not talking about hearing an audible response, and don't go thinking I've given you some special power. Anyone can hear me if they just will. You don't need to experience an angelic visitation to hear me; you simply need to listen—and not with self-focused superspirituality—just with quiet attention. I wish I could get that across clearly to all of my children. You do know how to hear me, whether you feel like you've heard my voice much recently or not. That's why you're writing this book—and why I'm letting you do it."

I contemplate this, trying to come up with a properly reverent response. "I do consider it an honor and a privilege to be writ—"

"Enough of that. Let's get back to the point," he interrupts. "The fact is that all those who really know me do know how to hear me—if they want to let themselves hear. My sheep hear my voice, you know? Whoever has ears to hear, let him hear. A lot of this 'Oh, I can't hear God!' moaning that goes on among my people is really a cloak for the fact that they are just too busy or too angry or too in love with the world to want to hear me."

"Lord!" I say with just a touch of (very respectful) protest. "This is . . . harsh! People who have picked up this book want to be comforted, not scold—"

"You don't think it's comforting that I am always here, listening?" God asks me, and now his tone is tender as well as urgent, embracing as well as bracing. "I am the lingering listener. I hear every prayer of every heart, waiting for my people to seek me, to talk to me, to enter into true relationship with me! That's why I made you, don't you realize that?"

"I know that's what you've said in your Book—"

"And there's another thing. Haven't you ever wondered why people whine about not hearing my voice when I have laid out so much for you right there in black and white? Think of it this way: I listen to you speak, I write you a letter, I wait to hear from you, and I long to answer your questions. Now if you would only open up to me and let me be for you who I am!"

"But, Lord," I reason aloud, doubt about this whole project beginning to chill me, "how can I be sure what I

21

hear is you? I mean, all of this might be coming straight from my imagination with absolutely no contact from you at all!"

"Is that what you believe?" God asks me.

I respond slowly: "No," I say, and it's not. I do believe the Lord speaks to me, that I can hear his voice, that I'm seeking to obey him, and that I am trying to write under the inspiration of his Spirit. Even so . . .

"Just for the moment," God says softly, "why don't you let your doubts go and just talk to me?"

"Okay," I respond. And here goes . . .

"You want to write a book that helps bring comfort to people by connecting or reconnecting them with me," he says.

"I do," I agree.

"And yet there are times when you yourself question my comforts and long for something more in life than what you experience daily."

"Well, yeah." I have to admit this is a part of my reason for writing these words. I want to grow closer to God, to experience a deepening of relationship to him. Oh, let's face it. I want to be blessed! Don't we all?

"Yes!" the Lord answers me. "Yes, you *all* do! That's why you talk to me. That's the nature of your prayers. 'Bless me, Lord, bless me!'"

"Umm . . . is . . . is that bad?" I ask.

"Of course not!" God responds. Do I hear a smile in his voice? "That's exactly what I want to do! I want to bless you! I want to allow you to experience the fullness of my blessings! I want to be in constant contact with you! Paul had it right when he said in 1 Thessalonians 5:17, 'Pray without ceasing.' I like that! I want to be in that constant relationship with you. And now—" God pauses, listening to my thoughts. "You're puzzling over a question."

God is right. (Well, of course he is!) What I'm puzzling over, however, is not a question I would necessarily put to him directly. It's something in the way of a criticism, actually. That's kind of embarrassing. But I realized long ago that I could keep no thoughts from him, so . . . "Well . . . Lord . . . um . . . if you really want us to remain in that close contact with you, then—"

"Then why don't I give you exactly what you want?" God fills in for me.

"Uh . . . well . . . yeah. That's what I was thinking . . . as you know. But, I mean—you're God! You can heal every disease, save every life, rescue every drowning man—"

"Grant every wish, fix every lottery, yeah, yeah, yeah," God responds.

I get the sense that my musings haven't pleased him—like I've missed a lesson somewhere that I should have learned by now. Still, since we're talking . . . "I realize I'm pushing it, but wouldn't that be granting blessings to us all?"

There's a pause. Has he stopped talking to me?

"No," God answers me firmly. "No, it wouldn't. It would be cursing you with meaningless bounty. Believe me, you wouldn't consider it a blessing at all after a time. You want to know how I know?"

I smile. "I figure because you know everything!"

"Because you don't appreciate your blessings right now," he says, cutting through my cockiness.

I gulp. "Well—"

"I have surrounded you with blessings that you take completely for granted," God says, and his tone isn't accusing, it's just . . . righteous. "I have blessed you with life. With an abundance of good things. Food, shelter, peace, a wonderful loving wife, a family that loves you, opportunities for service, gifts and skills, a great education, a marvelous nation to live in during a time of constant near-miraculous invention, far too much sugar, far too much emphasis on personal pleasure, far too *much* period. Oh yes, I've blessed you. But like every generation before you upon the earth, what you want is more *stuff*, not more me. And again, like every generation before you, what you fail to understand is that I am the blessing, not just the source of it."

Um . . . what can I say to that?

"How about 'Thank you'?"

"Thank you," I say weakly, but I know it's not enough. I feel like crawling into a hole and—

"Why would you want to run away from me when I've just told you that what I want is *you*?" God asks me gently.

"Because . . . I'm ashamed," I answer honestly. "When I think of my blessings . . ."

"What?" God asks me. "What do you think?"

"I . . . want to praise you!"

"That sounds about right," God answers, and for a moment I simply praise him for all he has blessed me with—not the least of those blessings being the opportunity to write these words of praise. As I start to turn my thoughts to other things, he says, "Are we done already?"

"Uh . . . done what?" I ask.

"Done talking."

"You mean, have I finished praying?" I ask, feeling a little guilty.

"Have you finished talking to me? Are you feeling 'all prayed up,' as some people say? Because I'd love to talk more."

"Well, yeah. I mean, since you're here and all."

"I'm always here."

"Yeah," I muse. "Well, okay. I'd like to ask you about some other things. That blessing thing—and other questions . . ."

"Go ahead."

"All right then, but some of these might sound impertinent!"

"Do you think I haven't heard far worse down throughout the course of human history?" he asks.

Does God joke? I wonder.

"Did I not create you in my own image," he asks, "and isn't humor a part of your nature?"

"Well, yeah, but—"

"Have I answered your first question?"

"About whether you hear my prayers? Yeah, I think so—"

"Then answer one for me. Are you going to keep *listening*, now?"

Gulp! I get the point of this. It's one thing to ask if God hears my prayers. It's quite another to say I'm always going to be listening when *he* opens the channel of communication first!

The fact is, I don't always listen to God, even though I know better. I have the scars and bruises to prove it. And I've been around churches and Christians from birth, so I've had plenty of opportunity to observe these behaviors in others. I've known a few folks I thought remained in constant contact with the Lord, but the truth of Scripture prevails: "All of us like sheep have gone astray. Each of us has turned to his own way" (Isa. 53:6). I'm afraid my own problem traces to a lack of prayer—of *substantial* prayer, not those pious-sounding prayer speeches we often pray in church (and which I've been guilty of praying myself). My own questions for God most often come from a lack of honest prayer—those times when I actually give attention to what my heavenly Father is trying to tell me. Jesus said that when we pray, we're to go into our prayer closet and talk to God privately. I think he was trying to tell us that this is where we can not only talk but listen, and so allow God to reshape our thinking.

I was taught to pray early—so early I can't even remember it. I was a preacher's kid, so it was expected of me. My family had daily devotions at the breakfast table, and my father called on each of us to close these sessions with prayer. Which meant that about one day in five I was called upon, and so I developed a rote prayer that popped out of my mouth automatically. It was kind of like pushing a button and getting a tape-recorded message. It started like that prayer with which this chapter begins: "Our heavenly Father, we thank thee for . . ." We all have prerecorded messages ready—when someone greets us, when the phone rings, when someone bumps into us or we into them, when somebody sneezes or says thank you. One night when I was about thirteen, my parents were out doing church visitation, and I was home alone. The phone rang, and when I answered it, somehow the wrong button got pushed. I answered, "Our heavenly Father, we thank thee for—" and then I stopped, embarrassed. "What?" said the voice at the other end of the line, and I cringed, for it was a sweet little lady from our church, who probably regarded me as a good little boy (I had *her* fooled, at least). I mumbled something, took her message, and got off the phone quickly. I'd learned a lesson though: what I called "prayer" *wasn't.* What was it? Good question.

It may have been around the same time that I learned another lesson from God about prayer. This time I really was praying for something, earnestly, silently—something I wanted for Christmas, I think, but I can't remember now what it was. We weren't well-off (preacher's kid, you know), and the only time we got any really big presents was at that blessed celebration time of the Lord's birth. (Strange—he has the birthday; we get the gifts.) So I was lobbying heaven for *stuff.* I was really trying to make my case, making this gift sound really good to God, when I overheard this thought tracking through my head: "How do I get God to give me what I want?" In that moment God spoke to me, saying, "Do you really think I can't hear you trying to manipulate me?" I heard no condemnation there, just a simple question from the Lord whose arm I was trying to twist. Ever since then I've known that silent prayer is dialogue with God—if you listen.

I love Ephesians. It may be my favorite book of the Bible (well, along with Acts, and John, and Jonah, and the list goes on!). The third chapter is a particular favorite. Paul begins to pray—publicly, so that the readers of this letter will overhear his conversation with God—and suddenly Paul interrupts himself to explain his credentials for saying these things and to launch into an excited, emotional praise to God for giving him, "the least of all the saints" (v. 8), the gift of being allowed to do ministry! I've often thought Paul never quite got that vision of Stephen going down under the rocks—or his responsibility for it—completely out of his mind. God had restored him, but I don't think Paul ever forgot his sin. Having established the purpose of his prayer to those he was praying for, Paul launched into it. "For this reason I bow my knees before the Father . . ."

What's the posture of your prayer? When I was a child I knelt beside my bed, and that posture is still an effective way of reminding me whom I'm addressing. At other times, the only appropriate prayer posture for me is flat on my face. When my wife and I were missionaries in Ogbomosho, Nigeria, we went to visit the *seaun* (that means "king") of the city. He greeted us with a handshake, offered us a warm Coke (that's how they drink it in Africa), and asked us to sit down. He had all these sofas surrounding the walls of his throne room. A moment later I was reminded that, to the people living in Ogbomosho, this was the *king*. A man came in to speak to him, and he *dobalied* before him. That is, he fell flat on his stomach, nose to the floor, arms extended before him. *Now* that *is how you greet a king*, I thought—then blushed to realize how little honor and respect I have sometimes shown *my* King when coming into his presence.

Then again, body posture isn't everything. When I was in college I played the evil King Claudius in *Hamlet*. In that play, Hamlet wants to kill his uncle Claudius, who has murdered his father, stolen his mother, and taken over the kingdom. Hamlet finds the evil king kneeling in prayer and puts away his dagger. He will not stab him while he's *praying*, for fear he'd send him straight to heaven! All right, so Shakespeare's theology may have been faulty. But the irony of the scene is this—and here I think the bard got it right—while Claudius is praying, he's not really praying, and he knows it. He mutters, "My words fly up—my thoughts remain below. Words without thoughts never to heaven go." His words serve as another reminder to me that it isn't the posture of the body but the posture of the *heart* that concerns our God.

Back to Ephesians. After Paul speaks of the posture of his prayer, he goes on to talk of its promise: "For this reason I bow my knees before the Father, from whom every family in heaven and on earth derives its name" (3:14–15). Do you see the promise I see? When we pray, we enter into the presence of the Father—the Maker—of *all*.

Think for a moment. We live on a planet that is ninety-three million miles from its star. The sun's light takes about eight minutes to get to us. The nearest neighboring star's light takes four *years* to reach us—it's that far away. Yet it and our sun are only two of two hundred billion such stars in our galaxy! Consider the immensity of God's creation! But, to go beyond that, our galaxy, unimaginably vast as it is, is only one of millions of such galaxies. How many? Scientists used to think about a hundred million. I honestly can't imagine that high. But then they put the Hubble telescope up and discovered they were off a bit: now they think there are five hundred million galaxies—five hundred million, each containing one hundred to three hundred billion stars each. Mind-boggling. C. S. Lewis said that if you can imagine all of that (impossible!) and then imagine it all the size of an acorn in the palm of our God's hand, then you might begin to approach in some small measure how truly great and awe inspiring our God really is. And that's the promise in Ephesians: this God, the Creator of all heaven and earth, gives us *personal* attention whenever we pray. *Wants* to give it to us! Seeks us out! And we wonder if he's able to hear our prayers?

Verses 16–19 give us the content of Paul's prayer for the Ephesians, and others, who would be reading his letter:

> That He would grant you, according to the riches of His glory, to be strengthened with power through His Spirit in the inner man, so that Christ may dwell in your hearts through faith; and that you, being rooted and grounded in love, may be able to comprehend with all the saints what is the breadth and length and height and depth, and to know the love of Christ which surpasses knowledge, that you may be filled up to all the fullness of God.
>
> Ephesians 3:16–19

Now, I may be wrong, but I see a pattern here—a pattern worth examining. I've sat in a lot of prayer meetings and listened as God's people created laundry lists of prayers. They were all important requests, of course, but unrelated to one another. This verse is no laundry list from which God might pick and choose which requests he will answer. Paul was praying publicly, remember; he was teaching his readers as he shared this prayer, and what he lays out here (under the inspiration of the Spirit) is the learning curve for the mature Christian. Do you see it?

First, that God will initiate faith in all of Paul's readers. Salvation is by grace, we remember—God's Spirit quickening us to believe—not the result of any good works we might actually accomplish in our own power. Every spiritual insight we have, God has given us.

Second, that Christ might dwell in our hearts through faith. Salvation is by grace *through faith*—our faith response to God's free offering. Paul longed to see everyone make this decision. It is the central goal of evangelism. In Paul's prayer, this is a starting point, not the end event!

Third, that we be "rooted and grounded in love," and wouldn't it be wonderful if we all actually were? I grew up hearing table talk about all the fights and frustrations within churches, not just in my own, but in those in neighboring towns and throughout my home state as well. As I got older, I heard the same kind of discussions concerning churches nationwide, then worldwide—the bickering and backbiting of the blessed. Through my young eyes, I saw very little "rooting and grounding in love" among Christians. Once I was grown and realized how hard it is to actually become this way, I still found myself longing for a fellowship of the saints where love prevailed over judgmental attitudes, self-centeredness, spiritual pride . . . oh, why even go on down that road? Anyone who's been part of a church knows what I mean. And if Paul is laying out a pattern for spiritual growth, then a lot of church folks are stuck back at salvation, never having advanced past the first grade to real love. And that's terrible, since it seems we need to get this loving *ground* under us before we can go on to the next point.

Fourth, that we might be able to comprehend—with all the saints!—what is "the breadth and length and height and depth." I really think Paul was trying to express the total dimensionality of the faith here. Maybe he was pacing around his prison cell as he dictated the letter. I picture him gesturing like a child singing that old song: "Deep and wide, deep and wide, there's a fountain flowing deep and wide." There is, of course, that fountain,

31

and it is deep and wide and broad and tall and long and every other dimension we might imagine. But I don't think we can learn all this without first being grounded in love.

If we Christians did all learn it, the results would be incredible. We could then know the love of Christ, which goes way beyond all human possibility of so-called knowledge. Paul wanted always "to know him," and this is what he's praying for—that all his readers might come to know Christ not just in forgiveness but in fullness.

Paul knew how to pray. Paul knew that God was listening to this prayer and that God would answer this prayer—at least, insofar as his readers would allow themselves to be blessed by God. But how many of us actually allow ourselves to grow up in Christ to the place where we can experience the fullness of God? I'm afraid that the answer is not many, or else I think we'd be making a much bigger impression on our world for Christ Jesus.

I think we're hung up somewhere. I think we're hung up on getting God to give us what we want instead of letting him give us himself. I think we're hung up on our frustration about that. When it comes right down to it, I don't think we're really well grounded in love—love of God, love of others, love of our forgiven selves.

Long ago I heard a preacher joke that seems to apply here: A new preacher came to the church and preached his first sermon. It was on *love*. All the people loved it and told him so. The next week he preached on love again. The folks smiled and nodded and thanked him at the door. The third week he preached on love *again*, and people began to talk. When he preached on love the fourth Sunday in a row, the deacons came to see him. "Don't you know any sermons about anything but love?"

they demanded. "Sure," he replied. "When you start *doing* that one, we'll move on to something more."

Want to move on to something more with God? Talk to him—personally—and listen to him. Let him love you and let your love for him grow, and more dimensions of God's wonder and majesty and fullness will expand in your heart daily. I'm right here beside you, praying for that myself.

Model and Qualifier

God is the *lingering listener*. We all love to be listened to. We want others to hear what we say. The simple truth of honest prayer is that God *lingers* to listen to us. He's always there, always ready, never cutting us off before we're finished, never looking at his watch, never seeking an excuse to run away. And he will linger *eternally*, listening.

Think About

- "Pray without ceasing" (1 Thess. 5:17).
- "Devote yourselves to prayer, keeping alert in it with an attitude of thanksgiving" (Col. 4:2).
- "Therefore, confess your sins to one another, and pray for one another so that you may be healed. The effective prayer of a righteous man can accomplish much" (James 5:16).
- "This is the confidence which we have before Him, that, if we ask anything according to His will, He hears us" (1 John 5:14).

- Read also Psalm 4:3; Matthew 11:28–29; and John 13:34.

Stretch Your Thinking

Then they will call on me, but I will not answer;
They will seek me diligently but they will not find me,
Because they hated knowledge
And did not choose the fear of the LORD.
They would not accept my counsel,
They spurned all my reproof.

Proverbs 1:28–30

Discussion Questions

1. Are you honest with God when you pray? Are you honest with yourself? Do you enter into conversation with him as if with a good friend, ready to listen as well as talk, or do you have a memorized prayer ready to pull out and recite at a moment's notice?

2. We all believe that prayer works. A common cliché one hears around churches is "Prayer changes things" (although that's not in the Bible. I've had people ask me for its reference!). The question is, What does it change? Whom does it change? How does prayer work?

3. Can you hear God's voice? Can you give a specific example of when you have heard—or felt—God was speaking directly to you? Did you listen? Are you still listening?

4. Do you feel too guilty to talk honestly with God? If so, you're probably in need of the next chapter.

2

"WHO WILL DEFEND ME WHEN I STAND BEFORE GOD'S JUDGMENT?"

I'm ashamed of myself. I'm worried. I'm repentant. "Are you listening, Jesus?" I ask.

"I'm always listening." His voice is gentle, as always. It's comforting to know he is always there to hear my prayers, regardless of what I have done.

"I did it again," I confess. Did what? Sin, of course. And the Lord answers, "I know."

"I'm sorry . . ." It is true repentance on my part.

"I know that too."

"But how do you—" I begin.

"Because I know your heart." There's no way to lie to God. If he can hear silent prayers, he can certainly read my thoughts! And my *guilt*.

The terror comes. "What am I going to do?"

"About what?" he asks, still gently.

"Isn't the Father furious with me?"

"All sin makes the Father furious." His words are frank and convicting. I . . . stand convicted.

"Then I'm out of luck, aren't I?"

"There's no such thing as luck," the Lord reminds me.

"I mean, I'm dead."

"The consequence of any sin is death, yes." That's straight from Romans 6:23.

"Even if it's just a little one?" I find myself equivocating. I sound like I'm trying to be a lawyer. The trouble is, I would *never* pass the heavenly bar exam. None of us would.

"Sin is sin," the Lord says firmly. "You know that."

I *do* know that. Sin doesn't come in degrees of deadliness. It is *all* deadly. "So what am I going to say?" I respond.

"When?"

"When I stand before the Father, the righteous Judge?"

"Let me do the talking," my almighty attorney advises, and he *has* passed the heavenly bar. He's the only one who ever has.

"You?"

"Of course. I'll be representing you."

"You mean, like a court-appointed attorney?"

"No, like a *you*-appointed attorney. You did ask me to be your advocate, didn't you?"

"When I—"

"When you accepted me as your Lord. Whoever confesses me before men, that one I will confess before my Father in heaven."

"That's a part of the arrangement?"

"One of the most important parts." Here is the comfort: I have a qualified heavenly intercessor arguing my case before God. Actually, he won't be arguing *my* case, I remember . . .

And here in my heart are those feelings again: the sense of regret, of shame, of condemnation, of self-recrimination. "The prosecutor must have a terrible case built against me—"

"Believe me," my attorney tells me. "He does."

"But then what do I have to do?"

"Plead guilty."

"Plead *guilty*!" I wail. That goes *so* much against our human grain, doesn't it? And we come by it honestly. Didn't our earliest ancestors, Adam and Eve, immediately try to justify themselves when God caught them in sin?

My advocate's legal advice is clear and firmly stated. "Confess your sin."

"To you?"

"To me, to the Father—it's going to come out the same either way."

"That's what I'm worried about!"

"What?"

"How it's going to come out!" Let's face it. None of us wants *justice* from God. True *justice* from God would be unspeakable. "I mean . . . after I plead guilty, do I throw myself on the mercy of the court?"

"You already have."

That's true. Repeatedly. "But what if the Father decides against me?"

37

"The Father won't be listening to you; he'll be listening to me. I'm your lawyer, and I'm also your defense. I'll file your guilty verdict and ask for immediate sentencing."

"My sentence?" I choke. "And that will be . . . ?"

"Death."

"Death!" I know the outcome of this conversation. You probably do too. Still, the reality of what I *deserve* for my sin causes me to demand, "What good is a court-appointed lawyer if I'm just going to die!"

The Lord is not impressed by my pretrial theatrics. "You're not going to die. You're going to live—abundantly, eternally, joyfully." That's the promise . . . isn't it?

"But you just said—"

"You've already been executed. Or rather, I have been executed in your place. That's your defense. But why are we repeating all this?" the Lord asks, already knowing my answer. "You *know* all this. We've had this conversation before."

"Many times," I confess.

"Yes, many times."

"And yet we keep having it," I add sadly.

And the Lord speaks *his* mind to me: "I wish we didn't have to."

"I wish that too."

"I know."

"But how do you know that I—" I begin, and again he interrupts.

"I know your heart."

"Right," I answer, reassured. "Right. But . . . I'm just wondering . . ."

"Yes?"

"Is there some . . . limit? You know, a limit to the number of charges I can have against me before you quit being my defense?"

"Seventy times seven," the Lord says. That stops my heart! I'd expected a simple no!

"Wait a minute. I'm not good with multiplication. That's 490 times?" I start figuring up my life in my mind. "How many have I already had?"

"Who's counting?" the Lord asks me. And I understand. I mean, I have failed him, I am certain, a lot more than 490 times. "And yet," the Lord continues softly, "here I am still. I didn't mean that as a limitation on forgiveness. In fact, I meant just the opposite. When I said that to Peter, he knew I meant 'an infinite number.'"

"You mean, when you were telling him how many times he needed to forgive his brother?" It's in Matthew 18:22.

"Exactly," the Lord tells me. "And I'm not just your lawyer, remember. I'm your brother too. If I told Peter he needed to forgive his brother an infinite number of times, why would I do otherwise?"

"That's comforting."

"I mean it to be." This is one of the most comforting aspects of our God—that he *intends* to bring us comfort.

But my self-condemnation still worries. "It's just that . . ."

"Yes?"

"Well, I just keep doing it. Sinning, I mean. And it's the same thing over and over!"

The Lord's reply to me is curt. "Most sinning is not very creative."

"It's . . . it's like I can't help myself!"

"You've got that right. You can't help yourself. But I can help you."

39

"That's just it! You know I've begged you again and again to help me not do it anymore, and still I—"

"Does that make your sin my fault?" the Lord asks.

It takes me a moment to catch the implications of his question. "What? No, of course not! I didn't mean that at all!" I didn't! (Did I?)

"You'd be surprised how many people use that argument with me. 'I asked God to help me, and he didn't!' some will say—as if that somehow justifies their continued disobedience!" Now the Lord sounds angry, and I am cringing. He has every right to be furious at such an inane idea. But he continues, "Let me tell you what it *does* mean. It means I will continue to forgive you as you repent and confess, and continue to help you to win this spiritual battle, insofar as you let me."

"Right," I agree, understanding him completely. "I mean, I know it's *my* fault when I fail to let you help me. It's just that . . ." I pause.

"It's just that what?" he asks, so patiently. How can he be so patient?

"Well, some people I've talked to say that after we've been saved, we're supposed to live in sinless perfection."

His answer is brisk. "Do *they* live in sinless perfection?"

"Well . . . I don't know. I mean, I don't know their hearts . . ."

"I do."

"And . . . do they?"

"Not if they're boasting about it to you, they're not! I inspired my good friend John to write something about that. John was always pretty blunt. People who say they have no sin are liars."

"Well, yeah, if they say they have no sin *before* they're saved, but afterward aren't we supposed to—"

"The prosecutor has really gotten to you, hasn't he?"

"The prosecutor?"

"The accuser. The one who would like to see you sharing his eternal misery. He's the one who condemns. I don't." He's talking about Satan, of course. I'm reminded of Revelation 12:10: "Now the salvation, and the power, and the kingdom of our God and the authority of His Christ have come, for the accuser of our brethren has been thrown down, he who accuses them before our God day and night." Still . . .

"But what about the Father? Won't he condemn me when he hears the accuser's case against me?"

"I've answered that. You know already that I and the Father are one! If you've seen me, you have seen the Father."

"So that means—"

"I'm not only your defense attorney; I'm the judge and jury as well."

Once again I breathe a sigh of relief. "Then . . . everything is all right? I'm safe?"

"From condemnation, yes. From hell, yes. I do have one question for *you* though . . ."

"I'll answer anything, Lord! After all you've done for me."

"You remember what I said to the woman who was caught in adultery, after everyone stopped accusing her in the face of their own sin?"

I think. "Ah . . . 'Go, and sin no more'?"

"You remembered. My question is this: why do you call me 'Lord! Lord!' but don't do the things I say?"

I'm thunderstruck. That's the real question, isn't it?

41

Is this the text of a literal dialogue I have had with the Lord? Would it ruin my credibility as a writer of a Christian book if I said yes? It's not, but it could be a composite of many conversations I have had with the Lord over the years, and it is honest.

Or at least it could be. The fact of the matter is that I have been a Christian so long that I more or less had come to take Christ's advocacy of believers for granted. Maybe you have too—maybe you are so secure in the love of Christ that this is not a question you ever find yourself asking.

But I have known a number of people—some of them longtime Christians—who have found this question a continuing problem. Saved by grace but very aware of their sinful natures, they have struggled and worried over such questions as "Can I fall from grace?" and "*Have* I fallen from grace?" This dialogue doesn't address this issue directly. It does, however, address the basic promise of the comforting words of God concerning our sin. That is, we're forgiven. Which I think *ought* to answer that other question about the eternal nature of our salvation.

God loves us. God loves us so much he provided a way of escape from the consequences of our sin, from the justice of his own wrath. Jesus announced it to Nicodemus one night on a rooftop, and the apostle John wrote down the words for us to read in his Gospel. God sent his Son into the world not to condemn the world but to save the world. Our salvation is not dependent on our doing. It is dependent on God's doing and on God's grace.

There is comfort here for the sinner. While Scripture makes it clear that the word *sinner* includes all of us, it also reveals clearly that God has himself solved the problem. Christ has already—of his own choice—paid the penalty for our sin, suffered the required sentence of death, and acts as our defense attorney. There *is* a legal stipulation though: we need to plead guilty. We *are* guilty, of course, but we need to enter that plea with the Father through our repentance and our confession. Then our lawyer, our advocate, the one who intercedes for us—our Lord Jesus Christ—is authorized to represent us.

He does more than that, of course—has already *done* it, actually. His sacrifice on the cross is the propitiation for our sins and for those of the whole world. *Propitiation* is a big word that refers to the sacrifice made for sin: sin is covered over by the sacrifice. Another big word, *expiation*, is closely related to it, and theologians discuss among themselves the relative importance of each. Propitiation may carry the idea of calming God down—as if that were possible. Expiation seems to mean something that scrubs us clean—the cleansing away of our sin. This is the basis for that old hymn that says, "What can wash away my sin? Nothing but the blood of Jesus." Expiation is linked with another big word, *atonement*, which means to pay the price for something. Jesus has already served our legal sentence. We deserve death, and he has already died in our place. Theologians call this "substitutionary atonement," which is really a simple concept if you explain it clearly—one even a child can understand. I know I did when I was eight. While we are responsible for our sin, Christ has substituted his own perfect life in place of ours, paying the penalty for us. Case closed.

But is it closed? What if we sin again after we have been saved? (And who of us hasn't?) This, it seems to me, is where a lot of wonderful Christian people lose

43

the comfort of their salvation. If we sin again after our sins have been washed away, doesn't that mean we've lost our salvation and fallen from grace? If you want to get *really* frightened at this point, just read Hebrews 6:4–6! This Scripture says that if anyone has *truly* tasted salvation and then fallen away from it, there's no second chance—no opportunity to be restored to grace without Christ being crucified all over again. Emperor Constantine—the Roman emperor who (unfortunately!) opened the way for Christianity to become the established religion of the Roman Empire—would not allow himself to be baptized until he was on his deathbed. He didn't want there to be any possibility of this happening to him. I certainly wouldn't point to Constantine's beliefs as an example of healthy Christian doctrine.

The problem with this common fear is embedded right in the very phrase "falling from grace." Grace is a gift. God bestows his grace; we don't earn it. If our behavior cannot earn grace to begin with, how exactly can our further behavior then *lose* grace after God has given it? If salvation is "not of works, lest any man should boast," how could our works after salvation destroy it? Do we really imagine that the God who made us, loves us, and saves us doesn't understand the terrible spiritual struggle we continue to wage with the evil one? Paul wrote that wonderful statement in Romans 8:38–39: "For I am convinced that neither death, nor life, nor angels, nor principalities, nor things present, nor things to come, nor powers, nor height, nor depth, nor any other created thing, will be able to separate us from the love of God, which is in Christ Jesus our Lord." Did Paul include any legal footnote to this effect: "Oh, but be sure you don't let Satan ever trip you up again, because then you can separate yourself from God's love forever"? He didn't. Thank God.

Much of this dialogue is based on the letter of 1 John. I love John—the ambitious, temperamental young hater of Samaritans who became the apostle of love. Now, 1 John can be confusing. At one point John seems to be saying that no one who is in Christ Jesus can sin (chap. 1); at another point he says, "If anyone sins, we have an Advocate with the Father, Jesus Christ the righteous" (2:1). So which does he mean? It helps to understand that he was writing specifically to people called Gnostics—a name that basically means "know-it-alls." They separated their spiritual nature from their material bodies, saying that what the body did made no difference. The soul, then, couldn't sin—or so they thought. John called them liars. Some of these people had gotten so far down this road that they actually *encouraged* physical sinning! Their crazy notion was that since Jesus saves us from sin, to sin more regularly provides more opportunity for his forgiveness!

Now, that's a pretty stupid idea on the face of it. The trouble is, some Christians seem to live their lives in that same spirit. They sin hard and loud on Saturday night, knowing that they can get it right Sunday morning. These people make provision for sin; they leave the door open to temptation in case they might want to go that direction. These are people who presume on Christ's forgiveness. And John, the blunt apostle, wonders why these people *say* they abide in Christ but don't keep his commandments.

The real question we Christians need to be asking ourselves is not "Who will defend me when I stand before God's judgment?" It is certainly not "How much sin can I get away with as a Christian before God finally gets sick

45

of me?" It is "Why do I call him 'Lord, Lord' but don't do the things he has commanded?"

For those who might have taken the love of Christ for granted, have you asked yourself *that* question? If you have trouble talking honestly and directly with God through prayer, consider this: you really cannot experience the comfort of God's forgiveness until you choose to live your life seeking at all times to walk as Jesus Christ walked. You can claim this comfort if you are willing to say to God, "In love of you, Lord, I want to walk like Jesus!"

Model and Qualifier

Our Lord Jesus is the *almighty attorney*. We understand lawyers; there certainly are enough jokes about them! But should we get into legal trouble or have a dispute with someone that cannot be resolved any other way, we *want* an advocate trained in the law to stand up for us. Scripture says that Christ is our attorney, but he's not like an earthly lawyer, practicing a profession for pay. And he won't move on to other clients and leave us without representation. He is the *almighty* attorney—the one who will win every case he argues, not because of our innocence, but because of his. And we never need to fear that a higher court might reverse the verdict, for he is almighty. He *is* the court. What a relief!

Think About

- "My little children, I am writing these things to you that you may not sin. And if anyone sins, we have an Advocate with the Father, Jesus Christ the righteous; and He Himself is the propitiation for our sins; and not for ours only, but also for those of the whole world" (1 John 2:1–2).

- "Who will bring a charge against God's elect? God is the one who justifies; who is the one who condemns? Christ Jesus is He who died, yes, rather who was raised, who is at the right hand of God, who also intercedes for us" (Rom. 8:33–34).

- "There is therefore now no condemnation for those who are in Christ Jesus" (Rom. 8:1).

- "For God did not send the Son into the world to judge the world, but that the world might be saved through Him. He who believes in Him is not judged; he who does not believe has been judged already, because he has not believed in the name of the only begotten Son of God" (John 3:17–18).

- Read also 1 John 1:8–9; 1 Timothy 2:5–6; and Hebrews 9:15.

Stretch Your Thinking

And why do you call Me, "Lord, Lord," and do not do what I say?

Luke 6:46

Discussion Questions

1. Lawyers sometimes get a bad reputation in our society. What does the concept of "attorney" mean to you? What does it mean if you qualify it with the word *almighty*?

2. Do you ever worry about doing something so bad that God cannot forgive you for it, no matter how much you may repent and confess? Do you know who it is that puts such condemning thoughts into your mind?

3. Do you believe it is possible to live in sinless perfection? Do you think the New Testament figures in the book of Acts and the Epistles demonstrated sinless perfection in all of their actions?

4. Do you think there is any difference between actually committing sin and making provision for sin—that is, leaving open a door of temptation in case you decide you want to sin again later?

3

"WHAT CAN I BASE
MY LIFE UPON?"

I'm a born Californian. I know earthquakes. I remember
a night when I woke to a distant rumble and found my
bed rolling across the floor of my fourth-floor dorm
room. Like the Californian I was, I just turned over and
went back to sleep.

But I've just experienced an earthquake unlike any I've
ever been through in my life. Not an earthly earthquake,
a spiritual earthquake. This is a *soulquake*. And my faith
in the bedrock of God's security has never been more in
doubt. So I talk to God:

"Lord, are you there?"

"You know I am."

"Then why do I feel so alone? Why do I feel like I'm falling? Why do I get the sense that I'm plunging off an infinitely high cliff and there's no spiritual safety net below to catch me?"

He's silent. Or at least, I don't hear him. Because that's the way it is when bedrock feels like quicksand—when foundation feels like foam rubber. God is hard to hear in those circumstances. I try again.

"Lord! Are you there?"

"As always."

"Then why do I feel like—"

"You've said this."

"Yeah!" I snap, "but you didn't answer!" There's anger in my tone. Resentment. Oh, let's just face it: I'm mad at God. I know my current circumstances are all my own fault, but he could do something about them!

"I guess you didn't read my letter to you," he says. And his tone isn't sharp at all.

"Which letter?" It's hard to keep the snarl out of my voice. I'm falling here!

"The long one—bound between the black covers. Well, usually. Sometimes now it's in paperback—"

"Father! How can you make jokes at a time like this?" I cry, and I recognize it's a helpless whine—the wailing of a two-year-old denied a toy in the supermarket checkout lane. I recognize it, I acknowledge it, but I can't help it.

And then God asks, "A time like what?"

It's hard to argue about time with God. He's not bound by it. He supersedes it. God made time, not the other way around. God owns time. Still, I try. "A time like now!"

His response is soft, soothing, a father's voice to a child who just doesn't get it. "You think I don't control *now* when I made every moment leading up to it?"

Okay. I have a choice here. I can hear him, or I can keep whining.

I keep whining!

"It's different for you! You don't understand what it's like to hang suspended in space while the seconds drag like hours, while—" (Wait . . . is that God *laughing* at me? I'm furious!) "Are you—!"

"It's just that what you've just described is what most people think is *all* I do."

"But—"

"Besides," he adds gently, "it seems I do remember something about hanging suspended between heaven and earth while the seconds dragged by like hours . . ."

"God!" I plead. My personal anguish in this moment is just too great for me to begin to think of *his*. "Father!" I beg. "Catch me!" And I cry helplessly.

His voice comes back with all the absolute certainty of the Maker of heaven and earth. "I already have."

"Are you certain of that?"

"Absolutely certain. The question is, are *you* certain?"

Yes. That *is* the question. Am I certain of God's . . . what? Existence? Care for me? Both? "Yes . . ." The trouble is I say this uncertainly. And God knows it. "But how can I know?" I plead.

"How can you know anything?"

I reflect. "From experience . . ." I begin. "From what I've been taught about thinking. From what I feel . . ." I pause.

"And what do you feel about me?" the Lord asks.

There is silence—this time from me, because I can answer God's question in so many ways. First I ask myself, *Is it* his *question? Is he there, or is this just my imagination talking?* Another way of answering would be "Lord, I believe—please help my unbelief!" After all, this is God I'm talking to. If he's *there*, that is. "Lord?"

"Still here. If you believe you hear me."

"You'll only be there if I believe?" I suddenly worry.

"Oh, I'm always here. But that's the only way you'll hear me. If you don't believe, if you don't trust, then how could you hear? You'll always be asking me, 'Are you there, Lord? Or are my prayers simply stopping at the ceiling?'"

"I bet you get a lot of that," I murmur.

"All the time," the Lord answers.

"Yeah." I could figure that. I know I've said it before. "So this hearing you thing. That's all dependent on my faith?"

"Of course. My Book says I'm here, and that I hear, and that I love you and care for you and . . . so much more. Why not read it again if you question?"

"I will Lord, I will," I say, for some reason delaying turning back to Scripture. "But first I just need to—"

"Think it over?" God interrupts.

"I guess."

"All right. So you've said you sometimes can't feel me. What do you think about me?"

God is pursuing me today. Aggressively. "I think . . . that . . . most of the time I believe you, but when I can't see the evidence of your salvation, I start to feel—"

"Wait, wait, wait!" the Lord interrupts. "You're back to feeling! I asked you what you *think*! What about the facts of my Word to you, taken by faith? Which comes first in all of this? My creation or your experience?"

Well, since God puts it *that* way, I answer, "Uh . . . your creation?"

"I think so! And what do you mean by the evidence of my salvation? Don't you really mean 'When things aren't going like I want them to, then God must not be there'?"

"Uh . . . yeah. I guess. That or . . ." I pause.

"Or what?" God prods me to respond.

"Why do I get the feeling that you've had this conversation millions of times before?"

"Because you've read Job, for one thing," God tells me, "and you know this has been a problem for every person who has lived. Now, this evidence you're talking about. That's what Job was asking for too. And he was basing his understanding of the evidence on his personal circumstances."

"So that's . . . circumstantial evidence, right?" I say, smiling a little.

God just continues to pursue me. "And do you know how powerful circumstantial evidence is in a court of law?"

"Only from Court TV," I joke.

God still pursues me. Like an attorney. "And that is?"

"Not very powerful . . ."

"Not nearly as powerful as evidence based on clear sight and absolutely certain testimony."

"Uh, yeah," I respond, bothered by the way this is going. "But . . . Lord? Job is hard." And it is. God and Satan talk, and God boasts about his servant Job and lets Satan put Job to the test by stripping him of everything.

The picture of God it paints is . . . hard. There's no other way to say it.

"You think Job is hard for you?" God says. "Think how hard it was for Job!"

And of course, that's my problem with it. I start to speak, but God continues, answering my unvoiced question.

"One of the reasons I put that story in my Book was as a misery meter!"

"A what?"

"A meter to measure your misery against. You think you've got troubles? Measure them against Job's!"

"Okay," I acknowledge, finally warming to the debate, "but I have this problem. You loved Job, God! Or said you did!"

"Yes," God responds. After a moment, "And your point is?"

I thought it was obvious! "So why did you put him through all of that?"

Obviously God has been awaiting this question, which I'm sure every reader asks him when they read the book of Job. And yet there it is, included in the Bible at God's intention, right in front of the Psalms. And God answers, "Why did I include it? So I could tell you about Job and about just how proud I was of him! And how proud I am of you whenever you continue to believe me in the face of the enemy's torments."

The enemy. Satan. I could write a whole other book about that creature, but my questions here are for God. "So what clear sight and certain testimony did you give Job?" I ask—a bit combatively, I guess.

"Look around," God says. "You see that?"

"See what in particular, Lord?"

"Everything in general!" God responds. "Whatever you're looking at, I made that. Everything you see. Everything you walk on I made, everything you breathe I made—everything. Grab my Book and read it! Job 38:1 through 40:2! It was after that beloved servant of mine had told me just how angry he was at me. Well, and after Elihu got after him for it . . ."

I go away and read that passage again. And as I read, I see something in it this time I never saw before. "I've always read that as . . . rather harshly said, Lord," I murmur, amazed. "Could it be that you actually said this gently? Lovingly? Like a patient, all-knowing father to an angry, blustering son?"

"It's hard not to sound harsh when you're speaking out of a whirlwind!" God says, and did he smile at that? "I can tell you this. I did say it with love. As I say it to you now: here is the evidence of my reality; it's all around you. Now tell me, are you going to trust that? Or trust your fluctuating feelings instead?

I think for a moment. I know the right answer. I give it. "What can I say to you, Lord, but what Job said? 'I have heard of you by the hearing of the ear, but now I see you.' Therefore I repent, in sackcloth and ashes."

"Okay," God says. "That's a good answer. But I can see you there writing, remember, with a pen in your hand. And you're wearing a plaid shirt and khaki pants, so you can cut the bit about the sackcloth. Job actually was in the ashes when he said it. Here's what I want you to do: make it as clear as you can to all the eyes reading your book that my Word can be trusted—that you can all build your lives upon my promises."

"Okay," I respond, the dutiful writer. But I cannot resist quietly asking, "Now will you make me feel better?"

"Are we back to that?" God sighs. "Look. It's like this. I have the long view. I see all of your existence from start to finish. Do you really think that after billions of years spent in my presence, you will still be holding against me the way you feel in this tiny moment?"

"No," I acknowledge. *But the fact is I still live in the here and now*, I think to myself. Out of God's hearing? Yeah, right! Like he can hear my silent prayer but not my silent grumbling? "Sorry about that."

God is very forgiving. Isn't he always? He says, "Think about what Paul said in Romans 8:18: 'For I consider that the sufferings of this present time are not worthy to be compared with the glory that is to be revealed to us.'"

"Yes, Lord," I respond. But the fact is that at this moment I would rather be experiencing that ecstatic eternity than my momentary misery. And God knows it. Knows me. Knows my tears, knows my regrets, knows everything about me. And—wonder of wonders—in this moment, that knowledge does comfort me.

Because, you see, I have built my house on a rock. Jesus talked in Luke 6:47–49 about the man who built his house on the sand—and when the rains came down and the floods swept across the countryside, his house was washed away. But over there, Jesus said, was that man who had built his house upon the rock of Jesus's words—the rock of faith, of dependence on God, of recognition of the evidence of his power all around us—and all under us. *I stand upon the Builder's bedrock*, I think to myself, and the words of the song come immediately to mind: "On Christ the solid rock I stand; all other ground is sinking sand, all other ground is sinking sand." As someone who has built my life on that rock of my salvation—on that cornerstone of all creation—I wonder why I spend so many hours slogging around through the devil's quagmire.

This is another honest *composite* conversation I have had with God. Why I continue to have it I don't know— other than that my circumstances are often difficult and the evil one loves to use circumstantial evidence to frustrate my faith. But I will claim this comfort today and answer the question "What can I base my life upon?" with God's comfort of the Builder's bedrock. We know what bedrock is—certainly as opposed to trying to step through the mud. And this is the bedrock of the Builder himself—the Master Builder, who laid the foundations of the world when all the morning stars sang his praises together. I was tempted to use the term *believer's bedrock*, because only believers can feel it under us, but our focus should remain on the comforts of God and on the one who *provides* that comfort. While our faith opens this comfort to us, our faith does not create it. God *is*, and God cares. That's the point.

I've heard these questions discussed many times. It seems when people are in the midst of terrible struggles—especially believers—the question comes down to this little rhyming couplet: "Is God there, or does God care?" Most of the time people ask one question or the other. That is, some people, even those who say they believe, have no trouble believing that God loves them—if God exists. Others appear to have no question that God exists; they just question whether he cares about them. Whichever form the question takes, the root problem is the same, and I think it's the same question Job asks: why would God allow this to happen to me? The answer seems to be one or the other of these possibilities. If God is supposedly loving and I'm hurting so badly, then either there's no God at all or he has specifically excluded *me* from his loving care. In the midst of my own struggles, I've asked the question both ways, with the truth as expressed in Scripture sounding utterly inconsistent to me. In other words, I sometimes might find myself thinking, *God cannot exist and be loving and care about me specifically and yet allow me to go through this!*

It is far too trite to stand back and say, "Oh, don't worry, you'll see that God will take care of you." People sometimes do that—ministers, even—but such a response doesn't generate much comfort. Why? Because it's just as circumstantial an answer as the question. It says, "Wait a while, and God will give you what you want." You know what? That's not always true. Then, when our miserable circumstances don't change, this sweet, cloying, sugarcoated encouragement can become a very bitter *discomfort* indeed. Satan uses it against us regularly: "You see?" the evil one says, "either you're not worth God's caring about or it's all bogus! Look at your unchanged circumstances! These 'good' Christians aren't suffering like you are!" In the face of great pain and suffering, God's comfort doesn't rest in circumstances, and we are fools to suggest that it does.

If you've read Job, you know that after Satan was allowed to strip Job of everything, three "friends" came to "encourage" Job. Their encouragement basically consisted of doing the devil's work for him. They told Job he was suffering because he had sinned. "No one could suffer like this," they basically said, "unless God was furious at him." They came to help and stayed to judge. What I find terrible as I read these words is that I know I have done the same thing. Not intentionally, of course.

I don't think Job's friends intended to judge him. I think it was just their natural reaction in the face of the tragedy Job was experiencing—that and their unthought-through belief that they themselves deserved the good things they were experiencing. Sometimes we believers do that when we feel comfortable: we take pride in our delightful circumstances. We comfort ourselves with stuff and with accolades instead of depending on the comforts of God. Yet if you read between the lines as Job talks about how wonderfully everyone regarded him prior to his fall, it seems that Job too took comfort in his position. And the trouble with this—as we all know—is that none of us "deserves" God's blessing. One of the greatest of God's comforts is that we are what God has made us by grace, not what we have made ourselves. "For by grace you have been saved through faith; and that not of yourselves, it is the gift of God; . . . so that no one may boast" (Eph. 2:8–9). Of this we may be certain: if we trust in our circumstances, then we hover in the air like Wile E. Coyote over a bottomless chasm, waiting for a fall. Circumstances—as Job discovered—are subject to instant change.

But when I am suffering, I can just as easily hear what the friends say to Job and accept it, and attribute my feelings to my own failure. I can hear the devil tell me, "God is so angry, you can expect never to get back into his good graces!" That's because I know the truth of what Paul says—that we are all sinners (and Paul, incidentally, claims to be the chief!). The trouble with this view is that it is simply the flip side of the arrogance of Job's three friends. We are still evaluating the love of God on the basis of personal circumstances. But God says he loves us. God says he forgives us. Why, then, do we continue to judge ourselves as unworthy of God's love? We are biblically correct only when we do not judge others and when we accept God's forgiveness for ourselves.

We live in a day philosophers describe as "postmodern." You may have heard the word and not understood it, or you may have heard the word so much that you're sick of hearing it, or both! One thing it means, however, is that people in this day and age tend to trust their experience over everything else. To be honest, I think that has been true of every age. People of the past may not have been so up front and honest about it. We do each live within our own set of circumstances, and when they are difficult, we tend to question everything—what we believe, whom we believe, why, and if we should continue to believe it. But all of history, way back to Job, can give us back this answer: if you trust only your own experience, then you trust in nothing but *circumstances*—and those can change, and for no apparent reason. There's no bedrock there. Can you build your life on "existential reality"? Only with the sadness of having to believe that there is nothing to believe in at all. Maybe that's why in pictures those existential philosophers always seem to be wearing the expression of someone up to the neck in muck.

Instead, take comfort in the Builder's bedrock. God *is*, and God cares, even if our circumstances seem to suggest otherwise. If you question that, look at Job and see that God stuck a really difficult example of awful circumstances near the center of his Bible, as if to say to us, "Look at this. Trust *me* and not your circumstances—because I have the long view." Now, why would God have put that story in there if he didn't know we all sometimes wonder, *Why?*

Some questions about Job's story: Are you as miserable as Job was? (For the most part, we have to chorus back, "No.") Did God redeem Job? (Yes.) Has God promised in his Word to redeem us? (Yes.) If what God has promised is true, are the circumstances of this present world to be compared at all with what God has promised? (No.) Finally, do we have another good option as a foundation for our lives, other than God? Peter answered this one, when Jesus asked his disciples (after he stopped feeding folks for free and they left), "Will you too go away?" Peter responded, "Lord, to whom shall we go? You have words of eternal life" (John 6:68). Peter often stuck his foot in his mouth. This time he simply stuck his foot down deep into the muck and found the Builder's bedrock.

When I was in college my father bought a ten-acre field in central California, on which he intended to plant pecans. One problem: Under the layer of topsoil was what they call "hardpan"—dirt as hard as rock, and impossible for anything with deep roots to grow through. I remember a day—a long, long day—when Dad rented a manhole drill (used to drill holes in pavement!) to bore holes through the hardpan so that the pecan trees could grow roots down through it. The night before we were to drill in our field, it rained and rained and rained. The next morning we had ten acres of mud to drill—and Dad dragged that manhole drill through those ten acres with his tractor. My job was to follow the slipping and sliding drill on foot and stick a stake in the ground wherever it drilled a hole. The mud was so bad, that was the only way we would know where to plant a tree! I suppose one could go many different directions with an illustration like this—and I had all day slogging through that mud to think many of them up!—but one sticks with me: Al-

61

though I may be slogging through the mud of life, and my boots keep getting sucked off my feet, and I'm weary, and I'm frustrated at my father for putting me through all this, and I wonder if I'm going to sink down into the slime of circumstance and be swallowed up by the slime, still I know that beneath me lies the hardpan of God's certainty. I may not be able to see it. My circumstances may not appear to be changing. But the *Builder's bedrock* is there. And that's a comfort.

Model and Qualifier

We understand the concept of bedrock—a foundation of rock or some other substance to build stable buildings on. The eternal qualifier here is that the foundation of our faith is the Builder himself—the maker of heaven and earth, the eternal, unchanging Almighty. When this foundation is available to us, why would we ever choose to build our lives on the shifting sands of circumstances?

Think About

- "The stone which the builders rejected, this became the chief corner stone" (Mark 12:10).
- "For I am convinced that neither death, nor life, nor angels, nor principalities, nor things present, nor things to come, nor powers, nor height, nor depth, nor any other created thing, will be able to separate us from the love of God, which is in Christ Jesus our Lord" (Rom. 8:38–39).

- "For this reason I also suffer these things, but I am not ashamed; for I know whom I have believed and I am convinced that He is able to guard what I have entrusted to Him until that day" (2 Tim. 1:12).

- "For this is contained in Scripture: 'Behold I lay in Zion a choice stone, a precious corner stone, and he who believes in Him will not be disappointed'" (1 Pet. 2:6).

- Read also Proverbs 10:25; Luke 6:47–49; and John 6:68.

Stretch Your Thinking

> Then the LORD said to Job,
> "Will the faultfinder contend with the Almighty?
> Let him who reproves God answer it."
>
> Job 40:1–2

Discussion Questions

1. Another story in Scripture deals with walking through difficult circumstances: the story of Peter who, when walking on the water toward Christ, took his eyes off the Lord and began to sink. A different image, yes, but what are some similarities to the concept of focusing on your circumstances instead of on God's love?

2. Have you been taught that God wants nothing for his children but "health and wealth"? Do you know any Scriptures to back up that view? Does it match your own personal experience? Could this

viewpoint be any comfort at all to the poor or the suffering? Do you think God cares for them?

3. It's just a silly children's story, but what is the relationship between "The Three Little Pigs" and Jesus's parable of the house built on the sand and the house built on the rock? What lessons would that fairy tale urge us to learn, and have you learned them?

4. What would you say to someone whose difficult life circumstances have left them questioning the existence or the love of God?

4

"Who Is This Jesus, and What Does He Mean to Me?"

There's been a lot of conversation about Jesus lately—" I begin, and God breaks in . . .

"Right. Because of the movie."

"Well, yeah," I respond. *The Passion of the Christ* stimulated worldwide conversation about Jesus.

"And that's good, right?" God asks.

"Yes," I respond.

"But?"

"I didn't say 'but,'" I answer.

"Really?" God says. "I thought sure I heard you."

There he goes again, reading my thoughts . . .

"Okay," I confess, "it's this. It's the problem I have with any movie, or painting, or novel, or representation of Jesus I've ever seen, read, or heard. It's just not . . ." I pause, looking for the right word.

God doesn't supply it. He just waits on me.

". . . . mine," I finally finish, although I'm not fully certain that's exactly the right word I'm looking for.

"Then what do you mean, exactly?" God asks. "Because right now it sounds as if you want exclusive rights to represent me."

"Yeah," I say sourly. "I know that's what it sounds like. But that's not really what I mean. What I mean is, the only true picture of Jesus is in the words of the Scripture. That's the total revelation that we have, that we can trust. Every other representation of Jesus says more about the artist than it really does about *you*."

"Including this book you're writing about conversations with me?" God asks gently. But I'm ready for that, was anticipating it.

"Exactly what I mean, Lord. I'm very much aware that what I'm writing is an interpretation of you, not necessarily inspired by you. And that scares me sometimes."

"Why?" God asks, although surely he already knows.

"I don't want to misrepresent you. I don't want to mislead anyone concerning you. Sometimes it makes it . . . hard to write," I confess.

"Then maybe you need to remind yourself what you're doing—that you are simply trying to think about me on paper, through conversation, in a way that might help you and others understand me better. Do you think that's a bad thing?"

"I'm sure someone reading this will think so—"

"But others won't. Can we go ahead and talk about Jesus now without all this angst?"

"But that's my problem," I explain. "What one person sees in Scripture another does not, and a third doesn't read the Scripture at all but takes others' words for who Jesus is and what he means—what you mean—to all of us. I have no right to reinterpret you in my own image."

"Not in your own image, no," God agrees. "But don't you have as much right as anyone to seek to interpret me in *my* image? You know me personally, as your Savior and Lord. Only those who know me personally can interpret me accurately at all. So go ahead. How do you understand me, my child?"

"As . . . as 'the central figure of the human race,' for one thing."

"Yes, I like that poem too," God says.

"But that's certainly not all. Christ Jesus is the Alpha and Omega, the Beginning and the End—"

"Which is another way of saying that I extend beyond what Einstein might call the space-time continuum—that before the world was I am, and that I will always be. But that tends to be beyond the scope of most people. You might want to stick to the facts of the historical Jesus. That's part of the reason I came in flesh—so people could understand me personally."

"All right. Well, as a historical figure we know you almost exclusively from Christian Scripture, along with a few mentions in contemporary histories of the time you lived and a few other 'apocryphal' fragments—"

"Meaning no one knows who wrote those or whether they can be trusted to speak accurately of me, as I've made certain the Scriptures do."

"Right. So, taking the Scriptures literally, you are the ascended Lord who lived on earth for about thirty years at the beginning of the common era or AD, when

Rome ruled the Western world and the Jews were still the primary occupants of Judea. Many people followed you at various times in your public ministry, mostly because you provided healing miracles and sometimes fed crowds of people miraculously. You invested most of your time in teaching a small group of followers, or disciples, about the kingdom of God, and then told them they would carry this message to the world. You were attacked by the religious leaders of the day because they didn't understand how you fulfilled the prophecies concerning the coming Messiah—because they didn't recognize you for who you were. They arrested you, turned you over to the Roman governor and charged you with sedition, and finally succeeded in having the Roman authorities crucify you. But you maintained all along that no one could take your life from you, that you 'laid it down' of your own choosing and for your own purpose, and that you could, and would, take it up again. That purpose—*your* purpose—in giving up your life on the cross, was as a substitute sacrifice for the sins of everyone. Anyone who believes in you can have your sacrifice for his or her sins accepted by—well, by you, as God the Father!—in exchange for his or her own eternal death. At least that's what I understand Scripture to say."

"So you believe it," God says softly to me.

"Of course I believe it!" I answer, perhaps a little startled by the question!

"Because that is the ultimate purpose of the Scriptures you have quoted. These things were written that you might believe that Jesus is the Christ, the Messiah, the promised Son of God, and that believing, you might have life in my name."

"That's John 20:31," I say, as if God needs a proof-text from his own Book! "But . . ." I begin, then pause.

"Another but?" God asks.

"But if all this is so clear," I say, "—and I certainly think it is—"

"Yes?"

"Why is it so many so-called Christians seem to miss Jesus entirely?"

"By that you mean—"

"So many Christians are so into religion, or church, or legalism, or justice, or some other 'issue of importance to the culture' that they seem to miss that *life* you promise in your Word!"

"Ah. So now you're ready to give *your* interpretation of me?" God says, and I think he's smiling. Because I like to see Jesus as the life of the party!

I know. Jesus, the life of the party? That's not a description we would immediately associate with Jesus, we who were raised to think of the gut-wrenching anguish of the cross and the awe-inspiring supernatural reality of the resurrection. "The life of the party" speaks to us of a self-obsessed person seeking the attention of everyone present through acts of embarrassing foolishness—a clown. Jesus was no clown.

And yet think about it. If you gave a party and could invite anyone who'd ever lived to it—anyone you've ever wanted to talk to or come to know—wouldn't you want Jesus on that list? We're talking about the central figure of the human race, considered so even by people who scorn those of us who believe in him. If you had the chance, wouldn't you want Jesus at your party?

Read the Gospels looking for parties, and you'll find many. Publicans and Pharisees alike wanted Jesus in attendance. John's Gospel tells us that Jesus was a valued guest at a wedding feast in Cana, where at his mother's insistence he saved the bridegroom embarrassment by turning water into wine. He invited himself to Zacchaeus's house, providing the diminutive tax collector with a public forum for his very public conversion. A Pharisee named Simon invited Jesus to his house and was scandalized when a "common" woman entered the house and anointed Jesus's feet with her tears. Jesus used this "scandalous" act to teach Simon a lesson about forgiveness. Who present would ever forget that party!

Wherever Jesus went, a party followed, a moveable feast of thousands, whom he served as host on several occasions. Jesus himself spoke parables of parties given and parties skipped, of guest lists expanded to include everyone in sight, of an eternal wedding celebration, to which all who come to know him as Lord will ultimately be invited, and without question, Jesus Christ will be the life of *that* party.

Teddy Roosevelt's son once said, "My father wants to be the bride at every wedding and the corpse at every funeral." We may all know people so self-absorbed that they want to be the center of attention in any situation. Yet Jesus did not seek the spotlight; he simply *was* the light in every situation. Why?

Jesus was full of joy. For American Christians raised on a spiritual diet of dour Puritanism, this may not be immediately obvious. The Renaissance paintings of gentle Jesus, meek and mild have left on our culture a nearly indelible image of a weak, almost feminine man who appears a passive victim of his Father's will. The Scriptures, however, tell a different story. They reveal a vigorous public leader who walked all over Palestine (no task for the physically unfit!); who courageously stood his ground in verbal combat with the pompous religious authorities of his day and always won; who lived his brief life to the fullest, building life-changing relationships with all those who sought him out. The Gospels show us a joyful Jesus, strong and bold.

Why would he not be joyful? He knew clearly his purpose, and he pursued it with energy, demonstrating God's loving nature as much to those who hated him as to those who loved him. He spoke with brilliant clarity, telling simple stories anyone could enjoy, if not wholly grasp. His was the joy of telling the truth—the truth that makes us free. No wonder people wanted to invite him home, to eat beside him, to hear him talk, to be with him. Certainly there were some who invited Jesus to their parties to be seen with him; that appears to be part of the burden fame inflicts on the charismatic individual. But from what we read, apparently he used these invitations as opportunities to delve deeper with people, to ask questions that pierced their motivations and showed them themselves. The best example might be in Luke 7 in Jesus's gentle rebuke of Simon the Pharisee. Why had Simon invited Jesus? Not to honor him, evidently. In failing to welcome Jesus with respect, Simon demonstrated how little he really appreciated Jesus's presence in his home. When a known "sinful woman" risked being thrown out of the Pharisee's house even though she came to anoint Jesus, Christ used her, not as an example of "other people's sinfulness" (as the gathered Pharisees appeared ready to do), but as a demonstration of how we treat those we really care about and of how we ought to approach God.

How did Jesus say this to Simon? As a novice actor, I was taught the critical nature of "line readings"—that is, the way a line is said, the emphasis placed on the words. I remember one rehearsal when an actress kept getting the line right but the "reading" wrong. She was supposed to say, "How did he get there? Blimp?" Instead, she kept saying, "How did he get there, blimp?" The difference was subtle but important. Her line reading kept changing "blimp" from a mode of travel to a rather personal comment on another actor's size! In this same way, how we read Scripture can place different interpretations on its meaning. When I see this party scene at Simon the Pharisee's house acted out in my mind's eye, I don't visualize Jesus humiliating his host with a ponderous pronouncement delivered with a withering glare. I rather see him slyly leading Simon to self-judgment—publicly, pointedly, but also positively—with the clear wish that Simon might understand and change. As a director I have to wonder, what did the other people present in the room do when this happened? Did they gasp? Did they mutter smirking comments to one another? Did they laugh at Simon's embarrassment but get Jesus's point? Did they grind their teeth in frustration, even as they marveled at his ability to turn any occurrence into an opportunity for honest teaching about the nature of God? We know the conclusion the Pharisees eventually came to: that Jesus was far too charming, far too brilliant, far too loving to be allowed to live. They became convinced that if they didn't stop this juggernaut of joy, the whole world would go after Jesus. Not that they managed to do so. The joy of Jesus was contagious. It still is. Jesus is still the life of the party.

Did Jesus have a sense of humor? I've often agreed with those Christian humorists who say, "God must have a sense of humor, or else how could he have created me?" I think Jesus had a wonderful sense of humor and that it was part of the reason those crowds tracked him from place to place. While no stand-up comedian, he nevertheless wove exaggerations into his teaching that must have had his listeners grinning, even as they understood the serious message the illustration revealed. The image of a camel trying to get through the eye of a needle, for example, or someone with a log stuck in his eye trying to see to get a speck of dust out of the eye of another. Are those lines really funny? They can be, depending on how they are read. Many people see no humor at all when they read Shakespeare, but his plays are loaded with comedy. The best actor to portray the Savior's sense of humor has to be Bruce Marchiano in the four-hour Visual Bible production of *Matthew*. Using only the words of the Gospel itself, Marchiano shows a Jesus who enjoys telling the parables—who laughs as he preaches, who pours water over an unsuspecting listener then quickly embraces him, who rolls laughing on the ground in celebration with a leper he's just healed. To those accustomed to film portrayals of Jesus depicting him as distant and cerebral, this all may take some getting used to. But the viewer comes away from this series with a new understanding of the rich warmth of Jesus—a warmth that made him the central figure of any gathering he attended.

That warmth was personal, directed to all who came across his path. He had what some call "presence," others "charisma"—that gift of making people around him feel as if their words were truly valued and their circumstances understood. Have you ever been with some "important" person who gave you his or her undivided attention; who listened to you and you alone as you spoke; whose eyes seemed to bore into you while listening, as if to see the real you hiding behind the mask? That was the Jesus the woman of Samaria met at the well—not at all concerned with appearances but definitely concerned with her. That was the Jesus Nicodemus met on the rooftop, who answered questions before the cautious Pharisee could even ask them, and did so with such profound simplicity that Nicodemus was never the same. That was the Jesus who—as he was dying for all the sins of all humankind's sordid history—nevertheless had words of encouragement for a thief who hung dying beside him. That was the Jesus who truly was the life of the party.

This is the Jesus people long to meet today. A world hungry for the truth, made cynical by the steady stream of the media's lies, needs to know the joy of Jesus, the truth that will set them free. People who have heard from the church only the cold, hard message of God's judgment for so long that they are certain "God" and "fun" are opposites need to experience our Savior's embracing, forgiving smile. Everyone who is lost and heavy-laden—that is, everyone—needs to experience the surprising joy of the personal presence of Jesus Christ in their own lives, a presence that brings value and meaning to this otherwise meaningless existence. But how can they meet him unless we who know Jesus share the contagious joy the Lord has placed in our hearts? Will a sour, judgmental witness reach them? Unlikely. Like the Greeks who came to the feast saying, "We want to see Jesus," the world—whether or not it knows this—longs to see him. Are we sharing Jesus's presence in our lives?

It's coming—maybe soon. All of us who know Christ have received our invitations to the wedding supper of the Lamb. Now that's going to be some party! Isn't there someone you'd like to invite to come along?

Model and Qualifier

So then, is this last image—Jesus the life of the party—the model and qualifier I want us to focus on in thinking of Jesus? Only if we were to say he is the *everlasting life*, or something like that. Actually, we can apply so many models and qualifiers to Jesus—and will in the coming chapters—that no one image will suffice. But if there is *one* earthly model and eternal qualifier I want to make certain we apply to Jesus, it is this: Christ is the *substitute sacrifice*. That is my understanding of the heart of the Good News of the gospel—that Jesus Christ died for us on the cross, a substitute sacrifice for our sin, and as a result has opened heaven for us. Because he died, and because he "took up" his life again through the resurrection, we have the promise of forever. One great advantage to all that? I know that a time is coming when all of my questions for him will be answered—at his feet.

Think About

- "'But from now on the Son of Man will be seated at the right hand of the power of God.' And they all said, 'Are You the Son of God, then?' And He said to them, 'Yes, I am'" (Luke 22:69–70).

- "Jesus said to him, 'Have I been so long with you, and yet you have not come to know Me, Philip? He who has seen Me has seen the Father" (John 14:9).

- "Therefore be imitators of God, as beloved children; and walk in love, just as Christ also loved you, and gave Himself up for us, an offering and a sacrifice to God as a fragrant aroma" (Eph. 5:1–2).

- "And by common confession great is the mystery of godliness: He who was revealed in the flesh, was vindicated in the Spirit, seen by angels, proclaimed among the nations, believed on in the world, taken up in glory" (1 Tim. 3:16).

- Read also John 5:32–35 and Philippians 3:8.

Stretch Your Thinking

Jesus said to him, "Because you have seen Me, have you believed? Blessed are they who did not see, and yet believed."

John 20:29

Discussion Questions

1. Have you ever heard people say, "I think Jesus was a great man. I just don't think he was God's Son." How have you answered them? How would you answer them now?

2. There's a well-known poem called "One Solitary Life." You've probably read or heard it. Can you imagine what this world might be like now if there

had never been a Jesus? (Fortunately, Jesus was always God's plan!)

3. A medieval monk wrote a devotional book called *The Imitation of Christ.* Scripture calls for us to be imitators of Christ. How do you do that in your daily life? Or, do you do that?

4. What is Jesus Christ worth to you? Would you die for Christ? Those who have been killed for their faith down through the centuries have been called "martyrs," from a Greek word that actually means "witness." If you said you would die for Christ, do you prove that daily by witnessing to others of your faith in him?

5

"How Can God Know How Bad I Feel?"

I don't "know your pain." I do know that anyone who says they do is lying, either to you or—to give them the benefit of the doubt—to themselves. I don't know what has caused your pain, only that it's a loss of some kind. Perhaps it is the loss of someone you love—through death or some other form of separation. Perhaps it's the loss of someone you were—through your own failure, or someone else's failure, or someone else's meanness or thoughtlessness, or selfishness, or . . . well, you know and I don't. It could be the loss of something you expected or maybe just hoped for—a future in wreckage, a dream damaged beyond repair. Whether loss of life or of lifestyle, of once-experienced reality or never-realized dream—whatever the loss, the price is pain. Unbearable pain. I don't know your pain, but I know my own.

Let me see if I can describe how it feels to me, and see if you recognize it. I hope you don't. I wouldn't wish it on anyone, not even those who played a part in causing my own. I think that anyone who bears a deep grief is in some way protective of it, and sometimes has a fierce kind of "You have no idea how bad I feel!" arrogance about it. But if you feel this—if you know what I'm talking about—then I'm talking to you. And in a moment I'll be talking to God for both of us.

I could say the pain comes in waves, but that's not quite accurate—not after a time, anyway. Rather, it comes in tides. When my loss first came, I was protected by shock. Wonderful thing, shock—like a body cast wrapped around your emotions. But that passed, as shock does, and then the loss, real and unchanged, stared me in the face. I wanted to die. I really did. Didn't want to kill myself; just wanted God to take me away. And here's what I have found most surprising: sometimes I still do.

They say that time heals all wounds. "How much time?" you demand as your own wounds gape open, oozing pain. "When you get through this," someone begins, and I interrupt to ask, "And when will that be, exactly?" Yeah, I've read the Kübler-Ross stuff on grief and its stages. They've apparently become canonical among the psychology community. There's denial, then anger, then bargaining, then depression, and finally acceptance. And I'm still sitting here asking, "When?" When will this pain be over?

The day after my sister-in-law died, my brother—who was also my best friend—asked me to take a walk with him around the block. Bless his heart—she had been ill for years, and he'd had plenty of time for anticipatory mourning. Didn't help though. You really can't "loss-proof" your life. Still, he had tried. And on that day I listened to him try to push himself through all five stages of grief before we got around the block and back to his house. There was no point in denial, he said; she was dead. So he would go on from there. Down one side of the street he raged. He was furious at God, and he let himself ventilate it. As we turned the corner, he began to bargain. Literally! Not, "God, if you will give me my wife back again, then I will . . ." No, rather he was bargaining with God to be a better father, pastor, and friend if God would allow the grief to pass quickly—like, right then! I just listened. I was his younger brother, not his elder; all I could do was walk beside him. But I fought my own tears as, on the third side of the block, he let himself tumble into the black pit of depression. Only for a block, however, for by the time we hit the next corner, he was moving on toward acceptance. Yes, he was accepting this—had been preparing for it a long time, right? As we headed up the driveway, he was utterly convinced that God had allowed him to pass already to the point of acceptance.

But of course, he hadn't. He never did get over the pain—not really. She died on Valentine's Day. Two years later, to the day, we buried my brother on Valentine's Day. We always have said that my brother Johnny died of a broken heart.

I also have not come to the place of acceptance, apparently, although some days I convince myself that I have. And because I have not, along with David in Psalm 13:1, I find myself crying out in the night, "How long O Lord? Will You forget me forever? How long will You hide Your face from me?" Because, you see, it still comes—the pain—like tides. I may go days without feeling it. Smiling, energetic, talking about it without apparent anguish, seeming to be "through" it. But I'm not through it. I wonder—with good reason—if I will ever be "through" this. Because it comes back, like the tide rolling in around me, overwhelming me, choking me, and it is every bit as bad—just as utterly unbearable—as it was on that first day.

Do you recognize this place where I dwell? Oh, I hope not. Because it was not always so for me. I remember days when I hadn't a care in the world, when I sailed through the hours meaninglessly, unhindered and unhurt. I say I remember those days; they hold a dreamlike quality for me now. "Was I ever really like that?" I ask myself. "Did I ever live in such an innocent—or perhaps I mean naïve—haze of blessedness?" I do remember seeing others in pain and thinking that I understood—thinking that a quick prayer over them and a benevolent smile upon leaving their presence would bless their day, yes sir! But I didn't know a thing about pain. How my clichéd benedictions must have sickened those who heard me. Or did they think I knew something they did not? I only know that at times I long to have that foggy foolishness back. Do you recognize these feelings? Do you mourn moments past? Do you know the acrid taste of regret?

If you do, you may remember a conversation with God similar to this. If not, let me voice it for you.

"God, please let me die," I plead. And I mean it.

He obviously didn't say yes. I'm here, after all, still writing these words. "I know you feel like you want to—" he begins.

"I don't just *feel* like it, Lord. I *long* for it. I'm ready to come on and be with you, where there's no pain and no heartache and no more tears. You're finished with me here, aren't you? Just let me come home to heaven, please?"

But he won't. He doesn't. And then it surfaces—that submerged feeling of hopeless, helpless anger that motivates my longing not to exist. "You have no idea how bad I feel, God! None at all!" Sometimes I scream this at him. Sometimes I snarl it. Sometimes it just sticks in my throat unspoken, creating a hot ache, the burning that precedes tears. Sometimes it doesn't even get up that far; it just hangs in my chest like an air bubble of lead—too heavy to get up, far too thick to pop—and all I can do is sigh. It doesn't help. I don't feel any better after I sigh. Just more weary than I can say. Can you identify with me here? Is this you?

"I can identify with you," God says.

"No, I wasn't talking with you just then, Lord. I was talking to the reader."

"But I can identify with you. I do know your pain."

Something inside me seizes up at those words. "How can you, Lord! I mean, with all due respect," I say (which is generally what we say whenever we're about to be really disrespectful), "you're God! You're . . . in control of all this! Aren't you? Because if you're not, I'd like to know who is!"

"Yes. I am."

"So how can you identify with me?" I snap. "I, who cannot control anything!"

"How can you presume to identify with your reader?" he asks.

"Now wait," I argue back. "If you've been listening to me, then you know I'm not presuming such—not at all! Instead, I've been saying all along, 'If you recognize this . . .'—not at all presuming that the reader will!"

"But why are you doing this? Why are you writing in this way? What are you attempting to accomplish by describing as clearly as possible your own emotional pain?"

"I want the reader to know how I feel—"

"Just so you can reveal your feelings? Get them off your chest, have your 'say,' so to speak?"

"No . . ." (I have to be careful here. There may be some of that going on inside me as I write. But honestly. . . .) "No. I'm describing how I feel so that if the reader understands—identifies—then I might somehow be of help."

"What kind of help?"

"The kind of help we people get from telling our hurts to those who understand!"

"I understand," God answers.

"Begging your pardon, Lord," I smile grimly, "but I really don't believe you do! You see, this is a people thing. If we can find someone to listen to us—really doesn't matter who, can even be a total stranger—who will let us simply unload how we feel, then we somehow feel better!"

"Why?"

I'm stumped there. "I don't know. That's just how we are."

"I know," God says.

"Yeah, well, you know everything, right?" I snap. "So why are we this way?"

"That's just how I made you," God answers me softly.

(Do you think it's terrible of me to rage against God this way? Haven't you ever? If not, I praise God for your joyful life and hope you never feel this way! But I happen to know that a lot of people do. And I remember a wise Christian brother, years ago, who told me to go ahead and be honest with God about my feelings—to yell at him, if need be. "David did!" he grinned. "And God's not going to fall off his throne if you do!")

"Let me ask you something," God inquires tenderly. "When you tell these things to these others—these strangers—and you feel better, does it last?"

Oh, now that's a powerful question. I've got to think about that. And of course, the honest answer is no. And God knows that, right? Otherwise, why would I be writing this with such ferocity?

"So then," God continues, "you have to find someone who is willing to listen to the same thing over and over again in order to feel better—or else find a steady supply of new persons to unload on. Right?"

I honestly don't know where this is going. "I guess so . . ."

"And you find that it helps you when you can tell someone whom you feel really does understand what you are feeling—someone who can identify with you."

"Yeah . . ."

"Which is why you are writing in this way—to establish to those readers who live with grief and pain that you are someone they can listen to and believe."

God's got me there. "I guess so," I acknowledge.

"And once you've won that reader's confidence—through conveying honestly the depth of your own pain—what then? What help can you offer?"

I think about that. "Not much, I guess."

"But I can," God reminds me.

"Can what?"

"I can offer real help," God tells me. "Real comfort. That's what you're writing about, isn't it? The comfort I can bring in the midst of your questions?"

"Well, yeah," I agree. "I mean, you could help any of us just by changing our life situations—"

"But that isn't what I'm talking about," God counters quickly. "I mean I can help by listening, with that same kind of identification you are offering! The 'been there, done that' comfort of the fellow griever! Because, listen to me, my child—my beloved child—whatever pain you have experienced, I have felt! Betrayal? I understand that kind of grief very well, believe me! Remember Judas? Denial? Just think of Peter, will you? Rejection? I am daily rejected, and not just by unbelievers but by those who claim me as Lord! Divorce? Reread Hosea, and understand through the writings of that prophet the depth of my grief in the face of adultery! Death? My child, every single day your world turns, I lose thousands of those I would long to call my own—people I love so much I would die for, and did—who slip off into eternal darkness without ever calling on me to save them. These whom I love are gone from me forever despite all that I could do. And you question whether I can understand your pain?"

"Wait . . . I—" I begin, embarrassed now by the arrogance of my anger. But God isn't finished with me yet!

"What do you think Isaiah meant when he said of me, 'Surely he has borne our griefs, and carried our sorrows?' Do you not understand that on the cross every single pain and grief and loss and failure of every person throughout the course of all human history was placed on my shoulders and mine alone?"

"Of course, but I—"

"Why do you think I made you so that you feel better when you unburden yourself of your grief? So you would come to me! So that you would share your burdens with me and let me take them from you! Which brings me to a question *I* want to ask of *you*."

Uh-oh, I think to myself. *Here it comes . . .*

"Why," God asks me, "do you insist on carrying these same burdens away from our conversations together? Why do you persist in continuing to bear burdens I could take from you? Do you know? Or do you want me to tell you?"

"Umm . . ." I'm afraid I do know, but I expect God is about to tell me anyway.

"Isn't it because you continue to swirl this bitter pill around in your mouth, hoping somehow it might yet become sweet?"

Now, that may sound excessively poetic, but the essence of what God is saying to me is clear: I'm resisting swallowing what has happened to cause me grief—bitter though it is. And the result is, quite naturally, bitterness. "All right," I say to God bitterly. "So how do I get this bitter taste of grief and disappointment out of my mouth? Just swallow it, I assume?"

"Stop cherishing it," God tells me.

"Cherishing it!" I snarl, certain that is far from what I've been doing, but God is ready for me.

"Just look it up," he says.

So I get the dictionary out and look up *cherish*. "To foster, tend, cultivate, protect, preserve, sustain, nurture, nourish, nurse, treasure, hold or keep dear, prize, cling to," it says.

"Oh," I say.

Interesting. Didn't say anything about "love," although love *is* something we cherish. Understandably. Why, though, do I protect, cling to, nurture—*cherish*—my grief?

"Because you still don't like the way things turned out?" God offers. "Because you think somehow by working it over again and again through your heart—wrenching though that may be—you might discover a way to change the outcome?"

That's insane. Someone once observed to me that a definition of madness is doing the same thing over and over again, while expecting a different result.

"It's not going to change," God tells me. "What's done is done. You, however, *can* change. If you'll let me change you."

"How?" I ask wearily.

"Give this back to me. Again."

Ah, there is the operative word! *Again.* For it seems I've given over this same grief to God again and again, and still I find myself—

"You keep taking it back," God observes quietly.

"Yeah," I acknowledge. "So how do I stop myself from doing that?"

"Cherish something else."

"What!"

"Cherish me."

Ah, yes. There it is. "Yeah. Well . . . that's . . . a little difficult right now, Lord."

"Because you're still angry at me for letting you suffer, and that causes you to continue cherishing your grief. So . . ."

"So . . . what?"

87

"Why don't we talk again when you're ready to stop cherishing it and cherish me instead?"

"Wait! Lord, don't leave me!"

"I'm not leaving," God reassures me. "I've told you I will never leave you. It's just that while you hold on to your disappointment, you can't see me. And it becomes difficult for you to see my blessings when you've become blind to what I'm doing for you daily. You see, my child, it's not for my benefit that you need to cherish me, to worship and hold on to me. It's for your own. But . . ."

"But what?" I ask anxiously.

"But I won't force you. I can only tell you that I've been there—I understand—and I can relieve you of your burden. But I won't make you give it up if you prefer to carry it yourself."

Now, one of the great difficulties of bitterness is if you've carried it a long time and for a long way, then—well, you've just got so much *invested* in it! It's really hard to surrender that, even if you don't want to keep it at all! Still . . . "All right, Lord. You know that ultimately I want to be happy and peaceful in you and that this burden is in the way. Again, will you carry it?"

And he does.

Model and Qualifier

Bible scholars have a particular name they assign the writings of Isaiah in chapters 40 and following, a name that Christians believe applies directly to Jesus: the *suffering servant* songs. They describe the one as-signed by God to bear our sin and be punished for our transgressions—a man of sorrows, one acquainted with grief. Jesus is that suffering servant, and this is the earthly model and heavenly qualifier for this chapter. Servant we understand: someone who serves others, generally of a lower estate in life. Jesus taught that any one of his disciples who would be "great among you" would need to become a servant, as he had (Matt. 20:26). The heavenly qualifier in this instance is *suffering*—and on an eternal scale. Jesus bore *all* the sins of *all* people in *all* history on the cross. When we can come to grasp the immensity of his sacrifice and also understand that he still wants to take upon himself our daily cares, then we're beginning to truly understand the nature of our God.

Think About

- "Sing praise to the LORD, you His godly ones, and give thanks to His holy name. For His anger is but for a moment, His favor is for a lifetime; weeping may last for the night, but a shout of joy comes in the morning" (Ps. 30:4–5).

- "Surely our griefs He Himself bore, and our sorrows He carried; yet we ourselves esteemed Him stricken, smitten of God, and afflicted. But He was pierced through for our transgressions, He was crushed for our iniquities; the chastening for our well-being fell upon Him, and by His scourging we are healed" (Isa. 53:4–5).

- "Jesus said to her, 'I am the resurrection and the life; he who believes in Me will live even if he dies, and everyone who lives and believes in Me will never die'" (John 11:25–26).

- "Bear one another's burdens, and thereby fulfill the law of Christ" (Gal. 6:2).
- Read also Psalm 14:6; Psalm 34:17–18; and Romans 8:22–23.

Stretch Your Thinking

Take My yoke upon you; and learn from Me, for I am gentle and humble in heart; and you will find rest for your souls. For My yoke is easy and My burden is light.

Matthew 11:29–30

Discussion Questions

1. Why do you think the concept of a "burden" is so easy to comprehend in any culture? What is the heaviest physical weight you have ever carried? Did carrying it wear you out as much as carrying some type of grief or sorrow?

2. Think privately of the greatest personal burden you are carrying right now. It may be your spiritual state, or some issue in your family, or some financial concern, but whatever its source, it is taking some emotional toll on you. Ask yourself, Is this a burden I need to be carrying? Is it a burden you haven't entrusted to God through prayer or that you have "taken back"? Can you surrender that burden to God right now?

3. In John Bunyan's famous spiritual allegory *Pilgrim's Progress*, the primary character, Christian, is on a journey to the celestial city. Only when Christian

reaches the foot of the cross and runs to embrace it do his "burdens" (a heavy pack he has been carrying on his back since the beginning of the book) fall away. How does the cross serve as a symbol of "burden removal" in your own life?

4. Ever watch a trail of ants carrying their "burdens" back to the anthill? They can bear enormous loads, and in our culture they have become symbols of industry (as opposed to grasshoppers, for example), which we have been urged by parents and teachers to emulate. Are you carrying any burdens out of some sense of antlike duty that really are not yours to bear? Do you get some kind of personal internal reward for carrying great weights that don't really belong to you? If so, do you really think God wants "good ants" in his kingdom?

6

"I WONDER HOW GOD WILL PUNISH ME FOR THAT?"

I'm eating pig slop!" I shout at myself with disgust, and I spew it out of my mouth like the garbage it is.

Filth! The spoiled, putrid, slime-encrusted leftovers from the bottom of the refrigerator! And why am I eating this again?

Now, that's simple enough. Because I've left my Father's table. *When did that happen*, I wonder?

"Are you asking me?" God inquires.

I hadn't been. Not exactly. Didn't want to face him with the garbage still dribbling down my chin. But that's the way of what we in church sometimes call "conviction." When confronted by our own failures, we're fully aware—again—that God is right there watching us. Has been all along. "I . . . I guess I am . . . ," I mumble.

"When do you last remember being at my table?" he asks.

"Not that long ago. This morning, I guess . . ."

"But you can't remember leaving it? Because sometimes people can. Sometimes they make a great show of leaving my table, unhappy with my provision."

Now, this stings a little bit, because I've had such moments myself. Yes, prodigal moments, when I've announced my intention to go off into a far country and waste everything? No, that isn't quite right, is it? We usually don't actually intend to squander our blessings somewhere; it just happens. And that wasn't the case this morning. No, it was just . . . slipping out of the chair, somehow . . .

"Turning your back on me?"

"Not consciously—"

"Taking me for granted?" the loving Father asks me.

"Not . . . consciously," I say again, as it registers with me that this is exactly what taking someone for granted means. I become very conscious, very urgent in my appeal. "Father, how do I prevent that from happening?"

"I would suppose," the Father tells me softly, "that first you need to *want* to keep that from happening."

"But I . . . I do . . ." Don't I?

"Do you?" God asks. "You set out in this chapter looking for my comfort as a forgiving Father. Why don't you go back to your initial image—to the prodigal in the pigsty—who 'came to himself'? Because I think that's what you are trying to do—'come to yourself' and face me—and to help your reader do that too. You never found that easy with your earthly father, so why would you expect to find it easy with me?"

Now, that's true. I had a hard time facing my father whenever I felt guilty. Went to great lengths to avoid doing just that. And here's the prodigal son in Jesus's parable, facedown in the pig trough, finally coming to himself and realizing that the effort *not* to face his father was far worse than the actual experience of facing him! How far down in the pig dung do we need to sink before realizing that? Pretty far, sometimes. And that's pretty foolish, given the picture of the forgiving Father that Jesus painted in his parable. Luke recorded it in Luke 15:11–32.

I wonder. Would the prodigal son have stayed in the slop so long if he had realized the welcome his father would offer him when he got home? I doubt it. I think he was expecting the worst and finally realized that the father's worst would be better than his current situation. "Even a servant is better off in my father's house," he reasoned, expecting, I guess, to actually be placed in the role of a servant in his own house when he got home. *Hoping* might be a better word. He was certainly not expecting *grace*.

Grace! What a glorious word! What a wonderful alternative to punishment! And yet so many of God's own stumbling, failing children do not know their own Father well enough to realize that grace is his answer to sin, not the destruction we certainly deserve for failing him. Grace is unmerited favor, undeserved care. Grace is God's decision to love us despite what we've done or allowed ourselves to fall into. Grace is God's constant offering to all who will come to him. And yet sometimes grace is hard to accept. Why is that?

"Because you think you deserve punishment?" God asks me.

"Ah, that might be it," I agree. "I mean, that's the nature of the world, isn't it? You do wrong, you get punished. That's even the basic outline of the whole structure of salvation, right? If we fail to accept your forgiveness, we receive eternal punishment in the fires of hell? Look, Lord—the whole of the Old Testament is filled with it—"

"But why direct your attention there? That was the old covenant—the covenant of law. Paul described the outcome of that system clearly in Romans. It's why I offered a whole new way of relating to me."

"Uh . . . yeah, but I guess I'm working here on your nature, you know? Scripture says that you are the same yesterday, today, and forever, so doesn't the Old Testament reveal you just as fully as the New?"

"My nature is unchanging. But by that argument, shouldn't you interpret my nature on the basis of the fullest understanding of it? When I sent my Son in the flesh in the person of Jesus, I was seeking to make myself more fully known than even the prophets could comprehend. I was no different, and—as you say—the message is no different. I want to be in relationship with my creation, and if you as my created child choose to run from me, then I will let you go—just as the father in the prodigal's story let his son run off and waste his treasure. But I've tried to make it abundantly clear through my Word that just as there will be judgment for those who ultimately refuse me, there is always grace for those who choose me. And if you read the Old Testament carefully, you will see grace in abundance there as well—grace to Jonah, who ran from my commands, grace to David, who sinned horribly but repented when Nathan confronted him, grace to my people Israel whenever they turned away from their pursuit of all the world offered and came back to worship me. Grace has always been in my character. Don't you see that? Why, then, would you insist on the need for punishment to set things right? Or is it that you feel somehow *justified* in punishment?"

"What do you mean, Lord?"

"Just this. Some people may feel that if they can 'do the time, they can do the crime.' Kind of a reverse entitlement. That their receiving punishment somehow balances out the eternal scales. It's as if they assume that experiencing punishment in themselves can save them, somehow, from feeling the weight of their own guilt."

"Okay, I understand that," I acknowledge. "I've known of people who sin Saturday night, then go to church on Sunday as penance, and feel much better if they hear a tongue-lashing sermon."

"Penance. There's the concept. And where in my Word do you find penance?"

I whip out my concordance. Actually, you can't really whip that book around; it's bulky and heavy—fifteen hundred plus pages. And between "pen" and "pence" I find no entry for "penance"—none at all.

"Uh . . . it's not here."

"And do you know why?"

"Because . . . it's really not possible for us to pay the penalty for our own sin? In any way?"

"If it were," God asks, "why would the cross have been necessary?"

And I remember again Isaiah 53:6: "All we like sheep have gone astray; we have turned every one to his own way; and the LORD hath laid on him the iniquity of us all" (KJV). All our sins have been canceled by the sacrifice of Christ—none by any penance or punishment we might have suffered. "So there's really nothing I can do to 'earn' my salvation through my own suffering, my own punishment . . ."

"Nothing. Nor any need. And anyone who thinks that somehow he can accumulate enough merit to win my favor through his good deeds is just as foolish as the one who thinks he can pay his own penalty for sin. My grace is your only hope. Of course, my grace is *plenty*!"

"And yet—" Here I go, venturing into territory I know God and I have covered before, "you allow us to suffer the consequences of our sin—"

"Sometimes," God corrects.

"Sometimes," I agree, for I can remember times when I thought I "got away" with things. Still, I press the point. "Isn't that punishment?"

"No," God tells me simply. "It is what you've properly called it—consequence. The natural outcome of a course of action. The prodigal son in the story had to get up and walk home, didn't he? You could call that a consequence. He'd traveled into a far country, spent everything he had, and was dirt poor on the trip home. Isn't that a consequence of his actions? Or would you count that as part of his punishment for his foolishness?"

"I might," I answer wryly. "Self-inflicted, perhaps—"

"But not inflicted by his father. His father was right there waiting—where his father always was—watching for his return."

"All right then, when we sin and repent we are not punished—exactly—but we suffer consequences of our actions. May I ask why others punish us so willingly?"

"Others being . . . ?"

97

"Well, other Christians, for example, who sometimes set out to punish us for our actions through their scorn or abuse or—"

"You're really talking about Christians here?" God asks. "Because that really doesn't sound like what I taught at all, does it?"

"Well, you did talk about weeping and gnashing of teeth—"

"In the outer darkness, where those who ultimately refuse my grace will go. But didn't I do that within the context of talking about my kingdom, where joy and forgiveness abounds?"

I try a different tack. "Well, Paul talks a lot about discipline—"

"Discipline!" God says. "Now that's different, isn't it?"

"Uh, how?" I ask.

"Discipline isn't punishment that somehow cancels sin. Discipline is training that turns a weak body strong. Discipline is for disciples—same root word, you know. It is for followers, to help them become more fit for the struggle. Paul said he pushed his body to make it more able to bear the weight of his work, and discipline is what strengthens muscles. But I really don't think that is what you're really trying to get at either."

"Then what is?" I ask, actually a bit afraid of the answer.

"Chastening," God says to me. "I think you need to get chastening and punishment separated in your mind. Think about that for a moment, and reread Hebrews 12:1–13."

"Okay," I say to God after I've reread this passage and reflected on it. "Yes, this is what I'm talking about. And

Lord, quite honestly, I can't tell much difference between what's described here and punishment—"

"Because it hurts."

"Yeah." That's the bottom line. Pain. "It hurts."

"But then you haven't read it carefully, down through verse 13."

"Oh, I have," I tell him. "I get it, Lord, I really do—that discipline is healing, that it's a sign of your love, and that through this we become partakers of your righteousness—"

"But it still hurts."

"Right. And . . . I guess, while I can see where it fits with grace, I don't see the prodigal son experiencing anything like *this* kind of discipline when he returns to the father—"

"You see no consequences in that story?" God asks me. "Think for a moment. Do you see him being restored to a level footing with his brother immediately?"

"His brother sure thought so—"

"Ah, his brother. But was that so? Not really. And wasn't his brother's attitude toward him a chastening consequence of his own behavior?"

"Maybe so," I agree, "but I think his brother was looking for more tangible retribution from his father!"

"Which is exactly why that story is so revealing of my nature," my forgiving Father tells me. "Oh, there are plenty of 'older brothers' among Christians today. I knew exactly who you meant a moment ago! Some of my children feel that I don't punish sin anywhere nearly enough and would happily volunteer for the job if only I would give it to them. Some merely take it upon themselves. The Pharisees were like that. Look at Luke 15:1–3, the passage that begins the 'lost' parables—including that of the lost son that we've been talking so much about. They were so busy judging others, they never did come to realize that they were lost themselves. And they are, even now, suffering the *consequences* of their own spiritual blindness."

I shiver at the thought. All those Pharisees, those who were so certain they knew what God intended that they missed the offering of his gift—now in hell. I shiver, because I wonder how many times I have judged my brothers, presuming upon my own spiritual superiority. "Judge not, you said," I murmur, not wanting to be guilty of judging others now. Not wanting to judge their treatment of me, not wanting to judge their relationship to God, I want only to get to that point where I can feel God's love and forgiveness in my *own* life and extend that gift to the hurting souls all around me who need it just as much as I do.

"Wanting to love me through loving others," God says, reading my heart.

"That's it," I agree. "That's where I want to be."

"And would you have gotten to this point without the discipline of walking through the consequences of your own failure?"

"Probably not," I answer, but the "probably" doesn't really belong there, and I know it. "No," I answer more honestly. "I can see that your discipline was necessary to get me to where I could experience again—how does that passage in Hebrews put it? . . . *the peaceful fruit of righteousness.*"

"Then why are you asking this question?" God asks.

"Which question?"

"The one that begins this chapter."

"Oh, right. The 'how will God punish me for this?' question. I guess the question really might better be

phrased, 'How are you going to *discipline* me for doing
. . . whatever?'"

"And the answer is . . .?" God prompts my spirit.

"Uh . . ." I try to sum it up in my mind. "You'll probably let me experience the natural consequences of my
bad choices, waiting and watching for me to realize I'm
back in the pig slop and to hit the road home. Then you
will welcome me back into your loving arms."

"So," God answers softly. "Are you ready to come
here?"

Am I ever!

And I can remember moments in my life of being
welcomed home—embraced and held by my parents or
my wife or my friends in a way that said, unequivocally,
"Oh, Bob. How I've missed you!"

That's how our forgiving Father embraces us when we
return to him from "a far country"—even while we still
smell like the pigsty. I cling to him. How I miss him when
I've wandered off! And in these moments I absolutely
cannot understand why I ever would wander off at all.
But then another thought occurs, and I whisper it in my
Father's ear: "But what about those 'older brothers' who
are looking on—who may be thinking I don't deserve to
be so warmly welcomed back?"

"Oh, my son," God answers me. "Do you think I've just
been waiting here for *you*? Don't spend any more of your
time thinking about them. Reread Hebrews 12:14–15
and make sure that you live as one fully forgiven and
free of bitterness."

"Pursue peace with all men," that Scripture says, "and
the sanctification without which no one will see the
Lord. See to it that no one comes short of the grace of God;
that no root of bitterness springing up causes trouble,

and by it many be defiled." *Whew*, I think. Understand, I've spent my life in churches, and all the bitterness I've seen between—

"Stop judging," God cuts me off.

"All right." That *was* bitterness in me, wasn't it? Oh, there's certainly justification for the thought. It's certainly true enough that many, maybe most, Christians do not live in this state of continuing love and forgiveness and peace with all men. But my job is not to judge them; that will only cause further bitterness. My job is to seek to help those around me experience this same peace God has given me in the wake of his discipline—and of his restoring love.

"Then how will *you* treat a 'younger brother' who has stumbled?" God asks me.

"Like I would want to be treated myself," I murmur quickly, for I've thought and prayed long and hard about this. I think that "Golden Rule" attitude is what is required of all of us if we are to fulfill Galatians 6:1: "Brethren, even if a man is caught in any trespass, you who are spiritual, restore such a one in a spirit of gentleness; each one looking to yourself, lest you too be tempted." Yes, I've been asking the wrong question. What I should be asking is, "What can I learn from these difficult experiences of life that will help me become more disciplined as a disciple?"

Can we be honest with ourselves? All of us have stumbled at some point or another. Some of us may even think we're getting away with it—that others around us think we're pretty holy, so we can continue to think that about ourselves. We may even find ourselves at times gathered with other "holy Joes," passing judgment on the fallen "younger brothers" around us. Of course, that's just another measure of our sinful nature, and Satan loves it. Thereby he divides Christians, divides churches—divides and conquers. I played football when I was young—played on losing teams, and then on one that won—and I saw clearly the difference between them. The losing teams weren't "teams" at all; they were clusters of small groups at odds with one another. I sure wish that didn't describe so many churches I've been in. I also know that you don't generate unity of the Spirit in a body by standing up in front of the group and shouting at them about how they aren't unified. I think the only way this unity happens—the only way I've ever seen it happen—is by first experiencing God's forgiving grace thoroughly yourself, and then extending it in every direction to his children who are around you. This chapter isn't really about punishment; it's about grace—grace that is greater than all our sin. This grace, this gift—this is what we are privileged to share with the world! I think if the world saw more of it *from* us—and more of it *among* us—then they would have a lot better understanding of what we are offering them through our witness.

I guess my real question for myself, then, would be this: Do people see God's grace in me? If they don't, what do I think I'm actually communicating to them about the nature of God?

Model and Qualifier

The model of this chapter has been that most frequently used model for God—the Father. Without question, many people in this world are not as fortunate as I was. I had a father who loved me and disciplined me in such a way that he modeled God's love for me. Even if you didn't have a father like mine, surely you've seen enough *good* fathers to know what the best of this model shows us. Jesus gave us this model himself in the prodigal son parable: the picture of the father that Jesus painted was drawn directly from his experience of the Father. The eternal qualifier here is *forgiving*—perhaps I should say *eternally forgiving*. For—in this life at least—Scripture says he will always forgive those who turn to him. It also says he will always discipline us to make us more like his Son and to give us peace. In other words, there's a price for the peace, and it's well worth paying.

Think About

- "Restore to me the joy of Your salvation, and sustain me with a willing spirit. Then I will teach transgressors Your ways, and sinners will be converted to You" (Ps. 51:12–13).
- "My son, do not reject the discipline of the Lord, or loathe His reproof, for whom the Lord loves He reproves, even as a father corrects the son in whom he delights" (Prov. 3:11–12).
- "Brethren, even if anyone is caught in any trespass, you who are spiritual, restore such a one in a spirit of gentleness; each one looking to yourself, so that you too will not be tempted" (Gal. 6:1).
- Read also Deuteronomy 8:5; Isaiah 57:18–19; and Matthew 18:21–22.

Stretch Your Thinking

Therefore let him who thinks he stands take heed that
he does not fall.

1 Corinthians 10:12

Do not be deceived, God is not mocked; for whatever a
man sows, this he will also reap.

Galatians 6:7

Discussion Questions

1. This chapter deals with the relationship between
   punishment, discipline, and chastening. Are those
   clearly separate concepts in your mind, or are they
   mixed up together? If they are mixed up together,
   ask yourself exactly what punishment God would
   need to extract from you to pay the penalty for your
   sin. (The Bible is really specific with the answer
   to that in Romans 6:23!)

2. Jonah received God's grace when he disobeyed God
   and was rescued from the sea (even if he did have to
   spend several days in a fish). David received God's
   grace when he repented of his sin with Bathsheba,
   but the child of their union died. Can you think of
   other consequences of sin biblical characters faced,
   even after being rescued and restored by God?

3. Is there unconfessed sin in your own life right
   now? When you read the passages above, were
   you feeling twinges of guilt—or, better put, conviction—concerning actions or practices or thoughts
   or behaviors or anything that might be standing
   between you and God? If so, is holding on to that

particular pig slop worth the separation from the forgiving Father it has caused you to suffer? Are you just afraid to face him?

4. You remember, don't you, the fairy tale of Pinocchio, the wooden puppet who became a real boy? Something like Jonah, he did some time in a whale as a consequence of his misbehavior before he learned about ethics and honesty and the impact of lies. Of course, Pinocchio's nose was a dead giveaway; it grew longer whenever he lied. Have you ever considered how long your own nose might be now if that very visible consequence were a spiritual law?

7

"WHO WILL TAKE CARE OF ME?"

I was preaching in a converted chicken coop. Everyone in the tiny village in western Zambia had become Christians, the direct result of Samson Sakala, the village headman, finding the Lord. They had cleaned out the chicken coop, thatched three sides and the roof, and installed split logs for benches. The day was hot, the place was full, and I was waxing eloquent about the nature of sheep.

I'm a city boy from Southern California. The closest I'd ever been to a sheep was in the San Diego petting zoo. But I'd read plenty, of course, and was young and full of myself, so I was explaining to these people the nature of sheep. As I did this, I looked out over their heads and watched a goat walk into one of their huts. These were pastoral people! They herded sheep, and goats as well! It suddenly struck me: What was *I* doing telling *them* about something they did every day? It was a great lesson for a young missionary about the difference between research and real life.

On the other hand, I *do* know something about sheep. The Bible says I am one—stupid, helpless, crowd-following, gullible—and gone astray. Forgive me for saying this, but you are too. "All of us *like sheep* have gone astray, each of us has turned to his own way" (Isa. 53:6, emphasis mine). And unlike Mary's little lamb who followed her mistress everywhere, we get lost from our Master regularly. A roaring lion seeks us out to devour us, and we cannot help ourselves. And some days, when the terrible reality of our own life situations hit each of us, we ask, "Who is going to take care of me?" Ever wonder why the Twenty-third Psalm is so beloved? Why people who are dying love to hear it read to them? Because no matter how secure we think we are in our position, no matter how safe we have made our dwelling place, no matter how much we've convinced ourselves that we've got it all under control, we haven't. No one has. And inside the proudest captain of industry or political ruler or fabulous movie star lives a little child who knows what it means to be alone and afraid.

"Lord, I'm frightened of the future. What will become of me? I don't control my own destiny. I am a child whose parent cannot protect me. I am afraid and insecure. Help me! I am lost! I'm—"

"Lost as in—how?" God asks me.

"Lost as in I don't know where I am or where to go to get back!"

"Back here?"

"Back—I don't know! Wherever it is I need to be!"

"Back . . . home?"

"That's it! Lord, take me home!"

"And where's home?"

I sigh. "If I knew that I wouldn't be lost," I mutter to myself, but of course God overhears.

"You realize, of course, that I know exactly where you are. Do you remember that Sunday morning when you were visiting the large church in Louisville?"

The memory floods back. The eleven o'clock service in a huge downtown church. I was between interim pastorates and we were visiting, seated in the steep balcony. The children's sermon had just ended, and we were watching the kids finding their way back to their seats—or trying. I was following the track of one blonde little girl as she climbed the balcony steps on the far side—and then the drama began to unfold. She was moving purposefully down the lower aisle when suddenly she froze. I saw the horror on her face. She was lost!

We were on the far side of the sanctuary, so I couldn't hear her cries, but I saw her tiny face screw up and tears begin to flow. And I could see her father. He was standing in the top row of the balcony, his eyes fixed on her, his arms spread open wide—doing everything short of shouting to her. An usher saw her, saw him, and quickly swooped in—a rescuing angel who restored her quickly to the safety of her father's arms.

Lost in church. I've often pondered the irony of that. How many of those adults seated in the congregation below me felt just as lost as that little girl, looking frantically for the Father, who was there all the time, watching and waiting.

109

I would like to be the usher who leads them to safety—but right at this moment I'm feeling just as lost as they.

"And I'm still right here," says the sheltering Shepherd to me, his welcoming arms open wide. For if I'm a sheep—and I am—then the Lord is my shepherd. I shall not want—

"But I do want, Lord! At this current moment I feel very much in want!"

"Oh, that I know," the Shepherd answers me softly. "And I know *what* you want. But why don't you just go on quoting those verses and see where they take you?"

"He makes me lie down in green pastures . . ." And my mind goes immediately to David, who wrote these words. When, I wonder? During what part of his long and eventful life? They were all drawn from his own shepherding experience, I know, but no shepherd boy wrote Psalm 23! Was he hiding in a cave from the murderous King Saul, longing for the safety of his father's fields in Bethlehem—before Goliath, before anyone knew his name—shivering in terror? Or was it the king who wrote these words—after Bathsheba, after Nathan pointed the finger at him and said, "Thou art the man"? Or was this written by the old king, pondering his days, recounting his mistakes, mourning Absalom—his own son—who had hunted him as murderously as Saul had during an attempted coup? Which David, I wonder, wrote the words of this glorious hymn?

"Does it matter?" the Shepherd asks me. "Does your wondering about David help you rest in green pastures? Because that's what I want you to do. To lie down and rest—under my watch."

"Like a child in kindergarten is forced to take a nap?" I had always resented that. Always had so much I wanted to *do* . . .

"And your *doing* is not what I'm interested in right now," says my Shepherd. "Your *resting*—your restoration—is."

"He leads me beside still waters," I think to myself, imagining that quiet walk beside a slow-moving stream. Sheep don't like to drink from fast-moving creeks. It scares them.

"And you don't need anything more to be afraid of right now," the Shepherd tells me gently.

He's providing clear water, rolling slowly through the green pastureland of my contemplations. Leading to "He restores my soul." Restore. Like reconstruction. Putting back together. Renewing—remaking my soul like new. Who is going to take care of me? Who but the Shepherd could handle that kind of reclamation project?

"He leads me in the paths of righteousness for his name's sake . . ." Again I think of David. He wasn't always righteous—

"Yet he was a man after my own heart."

"What does that mean, Lord?" I ask. "A man after your own heart? Because I want to be that kind of man, but my own heart is so fragile—"

"And David's wasn't?"

"Well, David was courageous, and—"

"Not always, believe me."

"All right then, David was loving in his relationships with other peop—"

"Oh, do you think so?" the Shepherd asks, reminding me of Uriah the Hittite, whom David in effect murdered, and of all that other blood on David's hands that prevented him from being privileged by God to build the temple. "Not always," the Shepherd repeats.

111

"Well, at least he was honest with himself. I mean—" (interrupting myself this time) "*most* of the time, anyway. But—not always?"

The Shepherd does not respond. There's no need to; for David had that same sin nature we all have, and that "always" level of perfection in righteousness *always* eluded him. "Then what made you call him a man after your own heart?"

"He always sought me. Like a bellwether sheep, he continued to lead others to seek my leadership and hear my voice. His words are leading you right now, aren't they?"

"*Your* words . . . ," I murmur.

"Written down through David's mind and experience. And when he strayed off, it didn't take much chastening or correction to get his attention again."

"Ah, yes," I say, smiling wryly. "Your rod and your staff—*comforting* him." This really is a strange metaphor. "The rod whacking the sheep over the head? This is comforting? How can that crook at the end of the shepherd's staff be comforting? It's shaped for the neck of a sheep, after all! Imagining that thing hooked around my neck giving me a quick jerk back into line just doesn't sound 'comfortable' at all!"

"And is comforting always *comfortable*? The staff was a symbol of authority and protection to David. With that same staff, David the shepherd boy fought off wolves— even a roaring lion." I understand the reference clearly. "But you've skipped a passage."

It's not a part of the psalm I particularly like. "Yes, even though I walk through the valley of the shadow of death." I tend to wonder—perhaps with most of Christ's sheep—why I have to pass through this valley at all.

Couldn't God just keep me out of that valley altogether? It's not the death part that bothers me. I know where I'm going when I die. But I have wandered through many kinds of shadowed valleys—sharp, rocky defiles—trembling in fear. Some valleys, to a Christian, can seem even worse than death.

"Which is why we're talking about this," the Shepherd says.

Yes. Fear. Whether it be a dark valley or a featureless desert, or adrift in a stormy ocean equipped with only a life jacket, whatever the image of fearful lostness, the feeling remains the same. Who will save me?

"We've established that," the Shepherd says.

"And when will rescue arrive—"

"There's the heart of the matter, isn't it?" says the Shepherd knowingly. "Your fears are not as much tied up in *who* will rescue you as they are in *when* and *how*."

I think about this. "Yeah," I finally admit.

"And the verse goes on to say?"

Dutifully I recite, "I will fear no evil."

"And why not?" the Shepherd prompts, but tenderly.

"For you are with me."

"I am indeed. Right here with you. Whenever one of my children asks the 'Who will take care of me?' question, the undergirding feeling is not 'who' or even 'if' I will rescue. The questions are 'when, where, how, and what will it cost me personally?' Understand: This is why my rod and staff get so much use. Because my sheep often want to run off into the future, when I'm concerned with now."

I smile. I'm remembering that common question from the backseat on a long journey: "Are we there yet?" And the driver's response—well, the kindly, *early* response anyway: "Not yet. Why not sit back and enjoy the view?"

As I was writing this, my wife and I caught the last two acts of Thornton Wilder's *Our Town* on television. You probably read it in high school. I once played the role of the stage manager—the crusty old narrator who comments on all the action and draws out the lessons for the audience to understand clearly. I was a boy when I played it. I knew all the lines but not all the *life*. Watching it with thirty-five years of experience now behind me, I finally got it. A young woman who has just died is given the chance to watch and participate again in an average day in her life. Weeping, she asks the stage manager, "Does anyone really see life—appreciate it—every, every day?" No. We don't. And here is what I "got" as I watched again, tears in my eyes: God wants us to live *each* day. He gives us today—and today, whatever our circumstances, we are to live as fully in his presence as we are able. We are to trust him for the future. We are to be sheep that follow, not ambitious apprentice shepherds of our own lives. We are to *live*—because that is what the Shepherd has come to give us. "The thief comes only to steal, and kill, and destroy; I came that they might have life, and might have it abundantly" (John 10:10–11).

And therein is my frequent problem. When I am not trusting my Shepherd, I can't see life at all. Not clearly. Not honestly, truthfully. Not what is real. And the evil one would love to keep me in that blindness. My eyes drift back to the verse on the page, what David (not King David, I realize at last, but *sheep* David!) saw as God's promise: "You prepare a table before me in the presence of my enemies. You have anointed my head with oil."

This is a symbol of blessing—God's blessing. And surely as he wrote these lines, David remembered Samuel's oil pouring down into his hair, over his ears and down his neck—the symbol of being chosen by God. "You did not choose Me, but I chose you" (John 15:16), Jesus said to his disciples. I know from this that I am not my own. I have been bought with a price by my Shepherd. A high price. He chose me! He's chosen you too.

"Surely goodness and mercy shall follow me all the days of my life." That's God's goodness, God's mercy, and more. Our English words don't quite sum it all up. That word *mercy* is also translated "loving-kindness." It's the Hebrew word *chesed* (pronounced "hesed"), and it is the best of the Old Testament words for describing what the New Testament calls *agape* love. David knew the true nature of God, for he had experienced again and again this wonderful mercy, kindness, and forgiveness. He knew it would follow him all the days of his . . . Wait. No, he *believed* it would follow him. That "surely" is a declaration of faith. "Surely his goodness and mercy . . . ," he wrote, as any of us would say of the uncertain future, "Surely such and such will happen!" We're sure, but we have to wait patiently to see it unfold, trusting in the Shepherd and not in ourselves.

One other word in this passage strikes me as curious— and causes me to smile: "will *follow* me," the Scripture says, and I think of the parent chasing after the impulsive toddler who keeps running headlong into trouble despite all the loving parent can do to prevent it or protect the child! Augustine wrote about God's relentless pursuit of us. The Shepherd will not give up on the straying sheep, but will hunt him down—restrain him, if necessary—in order to give him the needed comfort of his presence.

"What do you think?" Jesus asked. "If any man has a hundred sheep, and one of them has gone astray, does he not leave the ninety-nine on the mountains and go and search for the one that is straying?" (Matt. 18:12). David found comfort in this thought. There's comfort here for me too. If I wander away, God will chase me down. He already has.

"And I will dwell in the house of the Lord forever."

Are there any sweeter words? Maybe John 3:16, which explains the *how* of receiving this promise, but beyond that, there aren't many. This promise of God, understood and announced by David thousands of years ago, still comforts hearts in ways that surpass description. It opens up for me vistas of imagined blessing that are indescribably glorious—beyond my imagination, really. I shall be at home. I shall be eternally secure, eternally protected, eternally cared for. I shall be with those I love. I shall see again those I'm currently separated from, for as long as we choose to visit—in the presence of and under the smile of the Lord. This promise has no conditions attached, no cutoff date, no limiting boundary. Eternal life, eternal liberty, eternal happiness—this sentence promises all of that and more. Little wonder that people about to walk through the valley of the shadow of death love to hear it read aloud.

This is the answer to my question. This is who will take care of me. The sheltering Shepherd. True, I may spend my time worrying more about the how and the when, but those things are not in my control, and the Shepherd is scarcely going to put them there: he knows me too well. I'm a pretty dumb sheep.

The nice thing is that God knows that about me and knows exactly how to guide me. My job? To follow!

116

Model and Qualifier

The model and qualifier for this chapter? Simple—the *sheltering Shepherd*. The shepherd is a simple, well-known human image (even if few of us do this kind of work any longer), and the eternally sheltering, protecting modifier draws a picture of safety, security, and protection that pushes our imagination beyond our present circumstances to consider what it will be like to dwell in "the house of the LORD" forever.

Think About

- "Like a shepherd He will tend His flock, in His arm He will gather the lambs and carry them in His bosom; He will gently lead the nursing ewes" (Isa. 40:11).

- "Seeing the people, He felt compassion for them, because they were distressed and dispirited like sheep without a shepherd" (Matt. 9:36).

- "What do you think? If any man has a hundred sheep, and one of them has gone astray, does he not leave the ninety-nine on the mountains and go and search for the one that is straying? And if it turns out that he finds it, truly I say to you, he rejoices over it more than over the ninety-nine which have not gone astray. So it is not the will of your Father who is in heaven that one of these little ones perish" (Matt. 18:12–14).

- "I am the good shepherd; the good shepherd lays down His life for the sheep" (John 10:11).

- "For you were continually straying like sheep, but now you have returned to the Shepherd and Guardian of your souls" (1 Pet. 2:25).

117

- Read also 2 Timothy 1:12; Hebrews 13:20–21; and 1 Peter 5:4.

Stretch Your Thinking

All of us like sheep have gone astray, each of us has turned to his own way; but the LORD has caused the iniquity of us all to fall on Him.

Isaiah 53:6

Discussion Questions

1. The Bible is full of sheep and shepherds—from the flocks of Jacob in Genesis to those of David in 1 Samuel, to the shepherds abiding in the fields the night Jesus was born, recorded in Luke 2. This is not something we are too familiar with in our Western, industrialized culture. Still, many people reading Psalm 23 find immediate comfort in it without really knowing anything at all about sheep. Why do you think that is?

2. If you don't know much about sheep, it might be interesting to do a little research on this animal. Most commentary sets will expand on the nature of sheep either under the Twenty-third Psalm or John 10, and it really is enlightening to find how frequently the Scripture compares us to this dumb beast—and how well the comparison fits us sometimes.

3. The Psalms were the hymnbook of the Jews; they were all written to be sung. We have no record, of course, of the tune to which David sung the Twenty-third Psalm, but can you think of hymns and Chris-

118

tian songs that have made use of these images or phrases? How does singing these songs to yourself bring comfort in a troubled or anxious time?

4. One shepherding image Jesus used in Matthew 7:15 has entered popular culture—even into cartoons! It's the image of the "wolf in sheep's clothing." What is your understanding of what Jesus meant by this image? Do you know of any "wolves" in the present day who have clothed themselves as Christian "sheep" to prey on Christians? What should be done about them?

8

"Isn't There Any Other Way to God but Jesus?"

It just doesn't seem fair."

"What doesn't?" God asks me.

"That there is only one way to you."

"You want to talk about that?"

"It's a point of confusion for a lot of people."

"Fine. Let's talk. I'm right here."

"But why isn't that clear? So many people are trying to find their way to you—"

"And I'm right here, ready to listen."

"But they don't know how to reach you!"

"I'm right here. And my Word is widely distributed, even in secular bookstores—"

"But people don't know that."

"Oh, they know it's there," God answers. "They just don't *believe* it. And part of the reason they question it is this 'fairness doctrine' you seem to be puzzling over at the moment."

"Isn't it a legitimate question? I mean, think of all the people through the course of history who've tried to reach you in various ways—the ascetics, for example, who tried to come to know you by living a life devoid of pleasures—"

"Look at the world, my child! Look at the life I've made to be lived and the people I've made to be loved! Does it really make sense that one could reach me by denying that life completely, sitting motionless, waiting for me to speak? Yes, the Hindu mystics thought that was the way. Or rather, some of them did. Quite frankly, none of them ever agreed much on anything. Instead of arguing, they compromised and said there are many ways to reach me. All they really established was that there are many different ways to *try*."

"Why didn't you reveal yourself to them, then?" I ask, "In all fairness?"

"In all fairness," God responds to me calmly, "I *did*. I revealed myself to the whole world, and quite clearly."

"You mean through Christ Jesus—"

"I mean through the world itself. Paul made that clear, surely, in his preaching in Acts 14. He said clearly that I made 'the heaven and the earth and the sea, and all that is in them. In the generations gone by He permitted all the nations to go their own ways; and yet He did not leave Himself without witness, in that He did good and gave you rains from heaven and fruitful seasons, satisfying your hearts with food and gladness.'"

121

"All right, we call that natural revelation, and yes, I know you've revealed yourself that way to everyone, but why didn't you give them the *specific revelation* of yourself like the revelation you gave to the Jews?"

"Aren't you making a false assumption there?" God asks me.

"What false assumption?"

"That I *didn't* make my reality clear to anyone prior to coming in the flesh as Christ Jesus?"

I blink. "Well, you didn't. Did you?"

"What does Paul say in Romans 1? 'For the wrath of God is revealed from heaven against all ungodliness and unrighteousness of men who suppress the truth in unrighteousness, because that which is known about God is evident within them; for God made it evident to them. For since the creation of the world His invisible attributes, His eternal power and divine nature, have been clearly seen, being understood through what has been made, so that they are without excuse. For even though they knew God, they did not honor Him as God or give thanks; but they became futile in their speculations, and their foolish heart was darkened. Professing to be wise, they became fools, and exchanged the glory of the incorruptible God for an image in the form of corruptible man and of birds and four-footed animals and crawling creatures.'"

"Well . . . yeah," I flounder, "there's that . . . but—"

"But what?" God asks me, infinitely patient.

"But what about those who were genuinely trying to reach you and didn't know how?"

"Give me an example."

"All right, Gautama Buddha."

"The Buddha," God responds quietly. "Yes, he looked for me. But he never found me. In fact, he decided that I didn't exist and that the only way to achieve any peace of mind was to stop searching for me. Actually, to stop searching for anything. 'Desire nothing,' the Buddha said. But that's not the way I made you. I *made* you to desire a relationship with me. That's why people are in this quandary, don't you see? Why are you looking for me? Because I made you to want to know me. And then I provided the path for you to come to me—"

"Yes, but you didn't make that path clear to Buddha, did you?"

"My child," God says softly, "do you honestly believe you can judge how I have dealt with any other person down through the course of human history? Were you there?"

"Uh . . . no, of course not," I murmur, expecting God to start asking me the questions he asked Job in Job 38: "Where were you when I laid the foundation of the earth? Tell Me, if you have understanding, who set its measurements? Since you know. Or who stretched the line on it? On what were its bases sunk? Or who laid its cornerstone, when the morning stars sang together and all the sons of God shouted for joy?"

He doesn't though. Instead, he says, "You're asking this, I understand, out of a misguided human sense of 'fairness.' What you—and all those who ask me these questions—constantly seem to miss is that I have not tried to be fair, in human terms. If I had, all of you would have been destroyed long ago. Instead, I've always been loving. Just how loving I have been you'll not see until you stand in my presence at *my* judgment! But—for the sake of your 'fairness' argument—if you're going to try to argue that Buddha opened a 'path' to me, shouldn't you look at the outcome of Buddha's life? If he came to know me, why do you think he denied any god's existence? Why do you think it happened that some of his followers turned around and made Buddha himself into a god? Curious. And of course they built all those temples to him and constructed all those shrines, and his followers pray all those prayers to him. Doesn't my Word make it crystal clear that idols miss me completely?"

"Well, yes . . ."

"Buddha did not know me, and said he did not, and his followers pray instead to him through carved images. Am I to judge out of 'fairness' that they are actually worshiping me? Isn't that a bit like someone consistently dialing the wrong phone number—even though the right number is clearly published—and saying that it is not fair that I don't answer whatever number they are dialing?"

"Can I try another example?"

"All for the sake of fairness?" God says. "Go ahead."

"What about the Jews? Don't they know you?"

"That's a good question. You have my Word. What does it say about my chosen people?"

"Some of them knew you, surely . . ."

"Surely. And some of them?"

"Well . . . I guess some of them did *not* . . ."

"You don't need to guess, my child. That's pretty clear, I think, from the record."

"But doesn't that mean . . . some of them still could?"

"Who, for example?"

"I'm not talking about specific people, I'm talking about the pathway to you through the law."

"But I am *always* concerned with specific people. I am a personal God, not an abstract entity hanging out there in space somewhere. And the problem with my law is that none of my children could follow it. None, even of my best, could keep it. Not Abraham. Not Moses, to whom I gave the law. Not Samuel, who started out with me as a three-year-old. Not David, who was a man after my own heart. Not—"

"Well, of course, if you're talking about sinless perfection—"

"That's exactly what I'm talking about. That's the nature of law. Paul explained that to you. If you break any part of the law, you have broken the law. You don't have to transgress every law to break it. That's what I've defined as sin, and the wages of such sin is death. Now, before you jump in with some 'But that's not fair!' argument, remember, I *made* the law. I lived my earthly life in absolute accordance with that law and was sacrificed on the cross to provide you with forgiveness for your *personal* sin. That's not fairness, my child. That's grace."

"All right, Lord," I acknowledge him, "I recognize all of that, all that you have done for me, and I thank you and praise you for it. I'm just trying to figure out answers to some of these questions that others are asking me—"

"'In all fairness,' right?" God asks.

"Well, yeah, that's what they say . . ."

"Ask away," God says, but I can't help but feel he is really tired of this line of questioning from "fair" human beings.

"What about Muhammad? And those who call themselves 'Muslims,' which literally means they 'submit' to your will—"

"And regard my Book as full of inaccuracies, and follow another scripture that makes it a virtue to kill those who disagree with them, and regard my Son as the 'second most important' prophet—after Muhammad. Right?"

"Ah ... well ... that's the traditional Christian perspective, but—"

"But what?"

"But ... it ... just doesn't sound ... fair."

"Look at Islam itself closely, my child. It's the law all over again. There is no grace. There is no mercy. There is no love. There is no knowledge of me, only purported knowledge of my *will*—which, it turns out, is to deny the truth of my Word, hate those who believe it, and kill those who accept it. Does that strike you as being 'fair' in any human sense?"

"Not really."

"Then why bend over backward to call it what it is not?"

"Um ... because ... um ... politically ... uh ... that's—"

"Am I to assume we're no longer talking about what is true, but about what is 'correct'?"

"Let's change the subject then," I interject, still trying to be "fair" in human terms. "What about philosophy?"

"What about it?" God asks.

"Socrates, Plato, Aristotle—weren't they all looking for the way to become righteous men—or at any rate to live a righteous life?"

"And those who follow them are still looking. Quite unsuccessfully."

"It does seem, however, like the more recent philosophers have given up on that hope entirely."

"That's a bit of an understatement," God murmurs. Apparently he keeps up on philosophical trends—even when they don't much keep up on him. The whole so-called new postmodern thing is to pick and choose among all the religions and philosophies to find the things that you agree with and toss away the things you don't. Sort of a "do it yourself" religion. "Which is hardly new at all," God adds.

"I guess that's pretty much what New Age religion is too, isn't it?" I say. "A little of this, a little of that, with the basic assumption that if they all point to the same God, then they'll all get to you, right?"

"Sure, as if following every possible different road on a map will help you arrive at a single destination. Since when has that ever been true? Or is it simply not 'fair' that if one sets out in the wrong direction, he won't arrive where he wants to go? Think of all these world-views you've mentioned, 'in all fairness.' Which do you think might actually lead to me? Hinduism, which never reached me and never even made up its mind what it believed? The Buddha, who admitted to never finding me and then celebrated giving up the search by founding a new, godless religion? His followers—who turned him into a god? The Jews—who had my truth and then rejected it, crucifying their own Messiah in the process? Muhammad—who heard about me but decided he wanted to hear it in Arabic instead and wrote his own book? Socrates, Plato, Aristotle, and the rest—who tried to rationalize their way to me and never could, or their followers who had the truth told to them but preferred the constructions of their own minds to the simple faith I provided? Your postmodern friends—who are hungry to find me but want to be able to decide for themselves how to do it instead of letting me determine that? Do any of these ways sound like adequate paths to me—'in all fairness'?"

"Not really," I admit. "But then, those who would argue with that would say I only arrived at the destination I decided on to begin with . . ."

"With me, you mean?"

"Well, yeah, I believe so!"

"And how did you do that?"

"Um, through believing in Christ Jesus?"

"My child," God says. "If that's what you believe to be the only way to me, how could you possibly have arrived anywhere else?"

"But—"

"Yes?" God asks.

"I'm not convinced that what I've argued here will necessarily convince the person who doesn't believe you . . ."

"I'm almost certain it won't," God responds. "You came to me by faith, didn't you?"

"Yes . . ."

"That's simply the only way to get here," God tells me. And I realize that though I wish I could convince the whole world with arguments, what God says is true.

I have known God virtually all my life, meeting him as Samuel did when I was a very small boy. I honestly cannot remember a time in my life when I was not hearing what I believe to be his voice speaking to me. There was never a time I can remember that I didn't know the name of Jesus or know that Jesus loved me (I was, after all, singing "Jesus Loves Me" before I can recollect any conscious memory).

And yet I can stand by the veracity of this conversation. I have investigated each of these worldviews (that's what we call them now, rather than "world religions" or something else) with the purpose of understanding what the adherents of each seek to find in their belief, or their practice, or their assent. I started this investigation as a young man, and I'm well up there now. I've been trying to understand these things for a long time, and I've given a good chunk of my lifetime to teaching in these areas. What has struck me in all of these pursuits is this: how empty is the search for God himself, outside of the knowledge of him through Christ Jesus. May I be a little more specific? I'll tell you why in a minute.

Hinduism is not one religion; it's every religion. Every single religious practice or means of approaching God can be found somewhere in Hinduism, from a worship of a sacrificial God similar to our faith in Christ to a bloody, satanic ritual that we would equate immediately with devil worship. All of this comes under the umbrella term "Hinduism," which actually is a name given to these practices by Westerners long ago. It means "the religions of the Indus Valley," actually, and it covers everything that falls under the name of religion in India. There is no agreement, therefore, on what Hinduism is. That's why you may have heard people say that New Age religion is really Hinduism all over again. First, because many of the basic ideas of New Age (reincarnation, karma, Hare Krishna) come directly from Hinduism, and second, because New Age isn't one religious practice but all religious practices stuffed together into one bag with no single binding feature.

Then there is Buddhism, which has two main forms. One form follows the teachings of Buddha—which were, quite honestly, atheistic. Buddha never found a god to believe in. He then established a philosophy of life for people who wanted to be free from their psychic pain.

This was called the "eightfold path" and revolved around the central basic "truth" that if one could free oneself of all desire—that is, want nothing—then one could have it! Nothing, that is. The ultimate goal of the Buddha was to be in a nothing state—to get off the cycle of reincarnation and the pain of life so that he could be free of all pain. Odd, isn't it, how he believed in eternal life without God and wanted the nothingness of death, while Christians hold the opposite view—that only through God can we have eternal life and that we want it! And why is this important?

In the other form of Buddhism, Buddha's followers made *him* a god and began to worship him, asking him to save them. (It's interesting to note that this view, called Mahayana Buddhism, seems to have begun to spread around the first century AD, when the Christian gospel also began spreading around the world.) This worldview is different from classic Buddhism, called Theravada, and has some similarities to aspects of Christianity—salvation by grace being a most important one, a type of heaven being another—and an odd view of so-called Bodhisattvas that seems to mimic the Catholic view of the role of saints. All of this, however, is based on a man who didn't claim to be a god—who in fact didn't believe in God himself—and just wanted to go to "nothingness." (For those fans of a certain rock group, this is actually what "Nirvana" means.)

Then there is Judaism. The Scripture itself deals with this view. God fulfilled all of his Old Testament prophecies in Christ Jesus, and many of the Jews missed it. I said "many of the Jews," not all of them! The early church was an exclusively Jewish church and would have remained that way but for the efforts of the Jew named Paul and a number of other Jewish Christians, Peter an important one. Christianity is fulfilled Judaism, and for those who have been raised in the Jewish faith, it is the fullest expression of everything they have been taught—if they can manage to get the very gentile cultural trappings washed back off of it. The heart of the Christian faith is Jewish. What a shame that so many Jews are still missing what is essentially their own!

And then there is Islam. I've read the Koran. It isn't the Bible. It includes biblical characters, but they don't do things they did in the Bible. One of its most prominent figures—second in importance only to Muhammad—is "Isa," our Jesus. But Muhammad goes to great lengths in the Koran to say that Jesus never said what the Bible says he said about himself—that he is not the Son of God or the way to God, or other things the Bible says. The Koran is in direct contradiction of the biblical view of Jesus. It is also filled with scientific inaccuracies. Those who say that the Bible is scientifically inaccurate would have a field day with the Koran, but Muslims have never allowed it to be subjected to that kind of study by their own scholars. Those who tried were killed. The saddest thing about Islam, however, is that while it talks a lot about God, it does not seek to provide a way to know God. It supposedly reveals only the will of God (Allah, which is simply Arabic for God, and Arabic Bibles use the same word.) And the will of Allah is? Basically, to follow the law, as Muhammad laid it out—not dissimilar from the Jewish law and just as impossible to keep in perfection. Worst of all, the Koran knows nothing of God's love.

And then there are the philosophers—great minds, all—Immanuel Kant generally being regarded as the peak of philosophy. Kant argued for the existence of God but could not prove God even through the most powerful of logical constructions. Philosophy is marvelous and fascinating and awe-inspiring (if you like that kind of thing), but it ultimately fails as a means to know God. God didn't give us minds that could reason our way to him. He didn't need to. He'd already provided the means to come to him, through faith in Christ Jesus. There are a couple of other philosophical systems I've not mentioned—they come from the East, specifically from China—called Taoism and Confucianism. These are sometimes regarded as religions, but if you study them clearly, you see that they essentially are philosophies of living, not unlike those provided to the West in the same time period (600 BC) and equally unable to bring a person into relationship with the God who made us, who has said in Scripture that he wants to know us and wants us to know him and to have fellowship with him.

So why is all of this important? Because so many people around us today have never studied all these "ways," and they assume, not having studied them, that all ways lead to the same place. They don't. And that's important, because it means they really do not understand what it means to know God. And they suffer now the pain that Buddha suffered, of having a desire to understand but not being able to get there. And they will suffer forever the pain of being separated from God, when it is not his will that any should perish! (That's in 2 Pet. 3:9.)

All of this is of critical importance to those of us who do believe we know God, because the task he has set for us is to tell others what they don't know. By and large, we are *not* doing that. And I think that is in part because many Christians have bought the devil's line—in direct contradiction to the Scripture—that there are "many ways" to know God and that any of them are effective. That's dangerous! That particular lie will eternally be fatal to many people whom you call friends, or even family! It may be politically correct not to bring up the subject to them, but it is eternally incorrect for you to fail to do so!

The comfort of this chapter is: "Yes! There *is* a way for us to know God, and that is through Jesus Christ his Son!" What a comfort that should be to all of us who know him! If you don't know him yet, then accept the offering of Christ's sacrificial death on the cross as your means to salvation and come to know God today! And no, it is not difficult at all. A child could do it. I know. I did.

But there is a *dis*comfort in this chapter as well—or should be—if we are not busy about doing the task that our Lord has given us.

Model and Qualifier

The model of God in Christ alone that is pursued in this chapter could be phrased in many ways: Christ is the *one way*—*way* being the model and *one* being the eternal qualifier. That means, Christ is the only way, the unique road to God. Christ is the *divine door*—the only door through which we might actually have access to the divine God. Christ is the *perfect path*—perfect in life, perfect in purpose, perfect in universal applicability. But there is no other, imperfect path to God—only wrong directions.

133

Think About

- "Ask, and it shall be given to you; seek, and you will find; knock, and it will be opened to you. For everyone who asks receives, and he who seeks finds, and to him who knocks it will be opened" (Matt. 7:7–8).
- "For God so loved the world, that He gave His only begotten Son, that whoever believes in Him shall not perish, but have eternal life" (John 3:16).
- "I am the way, and the truth, and the life; no one comes to the Father but through Me" (John 14:6).
- "The Lord is not slow about His promise, as some count slowness, but is patient toward you, not wishing for any to perish but for all to come to repentance" (2 Pet. 3:9).
- Read also John 1:12; John 14:1–3; and Revelation 3:20.

Stretch Your Thinking

Then He will also say to those on His left, "Depart from Me, accursed ones, into the eternal fire which has been prepared for the devil and his angels."

Matthew 25:41

Discussion Questions

1. We live in a time when the concept of "ultimate truth" is widely disregarded, at least as applied to spiritual truths. The idea is something like "Truth is whatever you decide that it is." What would life

be like if this concept of truth were applied to law? To finances? To school? What areas of life today do you feel are already being negatively impacted by this attitude toward "ultimate truth"?

2. Some have asked, "Why would God only provide one way to himself?" Why do you think the question of fairness has become such a frequent—and apparently important—question in our present age?

3. If you were Satan and you were trying to invent a religion or philosophy that would prevent people from being able to see the truth of the gospel of Christ, what might it look like?

4. Are you certain enough of your faith in Christ Jesus to be able to defend your beliefs in debate? Do you think it is possible that at least some of the emphasis on fairness in our current culture is the result of Christians being too uncertain of what they actually believe to feel comfortable disagreeing with the views of others?

9

"HOW CAN I AVOID THE POWER OF EVIL?"

I watched a war unfold on my television. That's how wars are done these days—round-the-clock news coverage, split-screen images, a bulletin ticker running across the bottom. War as the ultimate "reality show." There's no way to miss a war anymore. It surrounds us.

And yet there is that other war that's under way, and is anybody covering it? That would be difficult, granted. It's invisible, so there are no good pictures. It's inaudible, except in our minds and hearts. The enemy observes no "rules of war," attacking secretly, sometimes in disguise. And I've been a casualty of that war before—my feet utterly cut from under me in a surprise attack—therefore I'm terrified.

"Lord?" I pray anxiously.

"I'm here," he answers.

"He's at me again. The enemy!"

"As he always is."

"But what can I do about it?"

"Besides what you're doing?"

I blink. "What am I doing?"

"Talking to me about it," God explains. "Because that's a pretty good starting place for resisting the enemy's attacks. He runs when you talk to me."

"That's right!" I remember, relieved. *Of course, I knew that already*, I congratulate myself. *Yep, I'm pretty well prepared for spiritual attack*, I think proudly—

"Don't go there!" God commands, and I jump with surprise. I mean, a moment ago I was in his favor, and now—

"Pride is the worst place to take refuge from the enemy!" he warns. "Whenever you think you're safe, you're not. Wherever you think you cannot be touched is precisely where you're the weakest!"

I hear these things from God, and I know they're true.

"Think of Peter," God continues, and in my mind I visualize that most trigger-tongued disciple at Caesarea Philippi. "But who do you say that I am?" Jesus had just asked them, and Peter—like the smartest kid in class firing off the answer before anyone else can get their hand up—said, "Thou art the Christ, the Son of the living God!" (In my imagination Peter seems to use "thees" and "thous.")

"Blessed are you, Simon Barjona," Jesus answered, "for flesh and blood has not revealed this unto you, but my father who is in heaven!" And Peter felt pretty good about getting an A on the pop quiz. A little too good? A little too proud? Because just moments later (two verses in the text), right after Jesus had begun to tell these guys what he had really come to do, Peter popped off again. And this time he got an F. "Not so, Lord!" he blustered—still in pride mode from the good feelings before—and Christ snapped him off, "Get thee behind me, Satan!"

Whew! "From "blessed" to "Satan" in a matter of moments—all by way of pride.

"I remember Peter, Lord," I say, thinking of these things.

"Then remember him weeping after denying me, because believe me, that's the incident *he* remembered." And in my heart, I know this to be true as well . . . what Peter recalled with pain all the rest of his life thereafter.

My wife and I have talked for hours on end about Peter's "fall." Looked at it many different ways. And this is her insight into it and into the spiritual war that is won or lost in prayer: "Jesus warned him at the Last Supper that he would deny him. 'Before the cock crows three times you will deny you ever knew me.' Then Jesus took the disciples out onto the Mount of Olives to pray with him. And did Peter? No. He slept through it!" Her point? Peter was too proud to believe he would actually deny Jesus. You can almost hear him smirking after Jesus warns him, as he thinks, *Lord, it'll never happen!* And while Jesus prayed for the cup to pass from him, Peter passed up the opportunity. Instead of praying for God to strengthen him in the face of the unknown battle to come, Peter relied on his own strength—and went to sleep.

"Sleeping disciples, Lord—that's what we all are, at times." And on this, the Lord makes no comment. "Of course," I add in quiet confession, "at other times we are wide awake and are still listening to temptation."

"Yes." Just that.

"Why, Lord? Why are we so . . . weak?"

"Because I made you that way."

Now that's true, but it's still surprising. Frustrating, even. "But why?" I demand.

"Because I am strong, and my strength is made perfect in your weakness."

"Second Corinthians 12:9, when Paul is talking about the thorn in the flesh," I respond. "Three times he prayed, asking you to take it away. And you didn't. I would have asked a lot more times than three!"

"You already have."

"Then why don't you take it away?" I ask again, earnestly. "Why don't you take away *all* our thorns in the flesh?"

"Because I want you to remain dependent on me. Because if I did, you would become satisfied with yourselves—proud—and move away from depending on me. Like Peter did. Like Paul knew he *would* have, and says so. Listen to me carefully: You are not the spiritual warrior! I am!"

I am. That's God's name in Hebrew, you know—"I AM that I AM." It's also "I was what I was, I will be what I will be," and every other combination of the "to be" verb you can think of. God is the same yesterday, today, and forever. But God is the spiritual warrior? "What about our part in spiritual warfare?" I ask.

"Your part," God tells me gently, "is to recognize your weakness and reach out to me for strength the moment you sense danger. You do that, and I'll give it! You fail to reach out to me, and I'll let you experience the consequences of your actions. Come out from under my protection, and the enemy will have you. That's not be-

139

cause I want it to be that way, but because apparently *you* do."

Now this is a stunning thought. Is it true? I mean, I've taught courses in spiritual warfare, and the current vogue is—

"To resist the devil and he will flee from you."

"Exactly!" I say to God.

"And how, exactly, do you expect to resist him in your own power?"

God knows my record here! "Not very well," I confess.

"Not at all," he reminds me.

Was this the barb Paul was squirming upon when he wrote about the thorn in the flesh? That he knew he had no righteousness in himself, and that—

"Are you asking me this or thinking aloud?" God asks me. "Because if you're asking me, the answer is, 'Of course!' Think about what he wrote in Romans 7! He's describing the weakness I built into your genes! And you know it."

I reread Romans 7:13–8:11. Now, I've heard some say that Paul was writing here out of *remembered* experience—that Paul no longer *had* such feelings, that he was just describing what he once felt. But I wonder. That really doesn't square with my own experience. Maybe it does with yours. But I wonder why he described these thoughts to the Christians in Rome if he didn't know that they would be able to identify with these feelings—only too well. Verse 8:5: "For those who are according to the flesh set their minds on the things of the flesh, but those who are according to the Spirit set their minds on the things of the Spirit." This is the dependence on God that makes his strength perfect in our weakness. It all depends on where we set our minds. A few pages over in Romans 12:2, Paul makes this even clearer: "Do not be conformed to this world, but be transformed by the renewing of your mind."

"So, this is a mind thing?" I ask God. "If I set my mind on you—"

"Then I will give you strength in the midst of spiritual attack."

"And . . . if I don't?"

"You know the answer to that."

I contemplate this. I know people who claim to live in a state of spiritual perfection, their minds always fixed on Christ. But as for me . . . "Oh, Lord!" I pray. "Protect me from these thoughts!"

"I am—while you are thinking of me." Almost as an afterthought, he adds, "Aren't I?"

"Yes," I acknowledge. "But what about after I put down my pen and close my notebook—what then?"

"Why, then you are still human, aren't you? Just like every other person reading these lines that you're writing, and you and they live with the moment-by-moment choice of whether to keep your mind fixed on me or not."

"But Lord!" I plead. "I'm writing about your comforts! Where is the comfort in admitting that I walk continually on the precipice? That we *all* do!"

"How about this?" God answers. "I'm here. I'm always here. And my strength is always available to you! Why complain that you live on a frightening battlefield, when ever since I saved you, you've known that is how things are? Why demand the comfort of my removing temptation from your life so that you can relax, when you know without question that not even my Son himself experienced that? Why grumble about your weakness, when I've made it so abundantly clear that you don't have to live there?"

There it is. The heart of what 1 Corinthians says about temptation: there is no evil we face that God does not provide us a means of escaping from, if we will just *take* that route when it is provided! "Okay," I say at last, understanding. "My longing for an ironclad protective security blanket is really—"

"A temptation to sin. To the sin of becoming spiritually proud—and no longer in need of my protection every moment of your life. Understand," God adds firmly, "I will not give you that comfort."

"But the real comfort is . . ."

"That I am always here. Always. Can't you take comfort in that?"

Is it enough? It has to be. Because this is the way God set it up. Our eternal security rests in him—his grace, his power, his presence in our lives. It does not rest in any way on us—on our works or our "righteousness." Good thing too, since we don't have any righteousness! God has it all. And yet he promises to be here with us, providing us with strength in any situation, with the power to resist any temptation, as long as we continue to be dependent on him for it each and every moment.

Oh, this is probably not the comfort we want. What I think we want is the instant cancellation of the spiritual battle—eternal rest and relaxation. And here's the good part: that's coming! One day we will see him coming in triumph, and this spiritual war with sin and death will be over. The devil will be toppled like a tinhorn dictator, his despotic rule over this world ended. That might happen today!

And it might not. If it doesn't, then we must remain in battle gear, living in dangerous discomfort in the field, eating spiritual MREs and longing for our true home. Paul spelled out the whole armor we need to put on for this situation—none of it our design, all of it provided by God. Our breastplate is his righteousness. Our loins are protected by his truth. Our shoes are the preparation of the gospel of his peace, our helmet is his salvation, our shield is the faith he gives us, our sword is his Word. All of this is in Ephesians 6:14–17, which is worth reading.

But whenever we talk about his armor, do we stop a verse too early? Verse 18 goes on to describe our need to stay alert in prayer. There's no metaphor provided for this—like "the spear of prayer" or some such. Perhaps that's because Paul recognized that prayer is our *means* of putting on this full bodysuit of protection. Our *only* means. I'm tempted to equate prayer with our spiritual underwear. It really is that—if you can handle the image without feeling I'm trivializing it. Believe me, I'm not.

How can I avoid the power of evil? I must focus my mind on God, drawing my strength from his power, doing so through prayer. This is certainly not as glorious a picture as visualizing ourselves as spiritual knights, out there doing battle with the demons while the saints around us look on and applaud our faithfulness. It is, however, a truer picture. Safer too. And more comforting. When Satan appears on our radar screens, clearly targeting us, we need to get into conversation with God. We don't have to protect ourselves from evil; God has made that his job. We just need to get behind him and let him do it. We need to have a close, continuing conversation going on at all times with the Holy Spirit. This is why

Paul said, "Pray without ceasing" (1 Thess. 5:17)—because the war is constant, and there are no battle lines to get behind. Satan, in effect, is a terrorist.

Where, then, do we experience the comfort of spiritual R and R? Is there no opportunity to rest in this battle? I think there is, although we often don't recognize it or give it its due. I believe that worship was designed to provide this place of consistent rest and refreshment. When God's people are together praising him, rejoicing in his goodness, recognizing his eternal victory over evil, we can find freedom from the battle. There is recreation in this celebration—a relief from the struggles of the battle and the pressures of the outside world. But how many of us truly feel that in church? I'm afraid many don't. And why not?

Is it because there is too much of the world in the church today? Too much temptation to sin through the ambition of achieving "pride of place"? Too much pride in our judgment of those "outsiders" who are not a part of our company, whom we regard with self-righteous arrogance? Too much competition to be regarded as saintliest or holiest or humblest or whatever? Understand, I grew up in church. I know what's inside those walls. Frankly, as a kid, I thought a lot of it stunk. I'm not seeking to be judgmental here, just honest, and I honestly believe that if the Lord were to walk into many churches today, he would pitch out much of what takes place, much as he did the money changers from the temple. I'm afraid that's the reason many of the "outsiders" of the world, the non-Christians, won't darken the doors of a church—because they have witnessed what goes on inside and determined that there is no spiritual comfort for them there.

Maybe this also is a part of it: In the necessary task of arming ourselves for spiritual battle, have we taken up the whole armor of God as if it *belonged* to us, was a kind of outcome of our own righteousness, and become too focused on ourselves as warriors? Has that caused us to judge, caused us to preen, caused us to compare ourselves with others and award ourselves top marks? Why, when sinners walk into some churches, do they feel the "saints" are mentally casting them out? Aren't we "saints" nothing but sinners saved by grace? The spiritual battle is raging. Perhaps you have not noticed, but an epidemic of "spiritual failure" exists among Christian leaders today. Figures say that seventy American churches close their doors every week, and while we are focusing much these days on planting churches, we cannot begin to plant enough to erase that deficit. This is with the population growing! All around us, a generation that has never experienced hearing the simple gospel of Jesus Christ in Sunday school (perhaps the first such generation of Americans?) is growing to adulthood. For the most part, the picture they have of Christians is one of self-righteous spiritual warriors who seem to take some kind of pride in condemning them as sinners.

Now, there is no chance that God will lose this spiritual war. It was won two millennia ago on the cross. But every lost *battle* consigns another of these postmodern pagans to hell. Can the church afford to be complacent and self-satisfied in the midst of such a war? Sometimes I wish we could see it on television. Then at least we would be constantly aware of it, and perhaps be praying about it daily. Then again, we *do* see it on television daily, don't we? The question then becomes, Are we praying daily about what to do?

Model and Qualifier

The earthly model for this chapter is the warrior—
Jesus. He is seen as a conquering hero. He has won the
victory over sin and death and will come at last to claim
his own. But God has not limited his spiritual conquest
to that accomplished in Christ on the cross. Through the
Holy Spirit, God remains eternally watchful over each
of us, ready to provide a way of escape from temptation,
ready to provide the strength to resist the devil, ready to
do battle for us in the face of our enemy. We may fancy
ourselves spiritual warriors, but we'd best remember
that it is God who is the *watchful warrior*. We need to
step behind him and let him wage the spiritual battle
on our behalf.

Think About

- "No temptation has overtaken you but such as is common to man; and God is faithful, who will not allow
  you to be tempted beyond what you are able, but with
  the temptation will provide the way of escape also,
  that you may be able to endure it" (1 Cor. 10:13).
- "But I am afraid that, as the serpent deceived Eve
  by his craftiness, your minds will be led astray from
  the simplicity and purity of devotion to Christ"
  (2 Cor. 11:3).
- "Therefore, take up the full armor of God, that you
  may be able to resist in the evil day, and having
  done everything, to stand firm" (Eph. 6:13).
- "Submit therefore to God. Resist the devil and he
  will flee from you" (James 4:7).

- "Be of sober spirit, be on the alert. Your adversary, the devil, prowls about like a roaring lion, seeking someone to devour. But resist him, firm in your faith, knowing that the same experiences of suffering are being accomplished by your brethren who are in the world" (1 Pet. 5:8–9).
- Read also Romans 6:12–13; 2 Corinthians 2:11; and James 1:2–3.

Stretch Your Thinking

You therefore, beloved, knowing this beforehand, be on your guard so that you are not carried away by the error of unprincipled men and fall from your own steadfastness.

2 Peter 3:17

Discussion Questions

1. The Christian market in recent years has seen an influx of books about spiritual warfare. Prior to that, there weren't many books at all. Do you think that's because ours is the first generation of Christians (recently, anyway) to be aware of the spiritual battle? Or do you think there might be some other reason for this phenomenon? If so, what would it be?
2. What spiritual battle rages in your own personal life? Does a particular sinful practice have a hold on you in some way that you've asked God to take away but still remains? Looking at the Scriptures given above, what part do you yourself need to play

147

in letting God cleanse you of unhealthy habits or thoughts?

3. The Scripture says that Satan is a liar and the father of lies. Is there any particular lie that Satan uses on you regularly, repeatedly, to trip you up or make you feel afraid or ashamed? Can you voice to yourself exactly what that lie is and let the Holy Spirit provide you with an answer to it?

4. Popular culture is filled with stories and movies of battles between good and evil, between "good" humans and evil spirits, between demonic forces and those stalwart few who stand for "truth, justice, and the American way." Have you given any thought to why such stories might be so fascinating to today's world? Do you think it might be that young people are hungry for news of a warrior who can actually protect them against the darkness of this present age?

10

"How Can One Person Make a Difference?"

Who am I to seek to change the world? I am flawed. I am weary. I know the needs; television, newspapers, movies, private conversations, all these tell me that the world is in a mess. I also know all those clichés: "If you're not part of the solution, you're part of the problem!" And that's the problem. I *am* part of the problem. I know what Scripture says is the solution: this world needs to come to know the God who loves it, who made it, who provided salvation—the only solution—through Christ Jesus. And I love Jesus. But how can I make any impression on this massive, cold, intimidating culture that now spans the world in an interconnected Web—this spider's web of electronic influence, this matrix of madness and mess?

I grew up in Los Angeles. We joke that my wife also grew up in L.A. That's what the natives call "lower Alabama." In lower Alabama, there is still a *manageable* size to the world. There is an outer coating, at least, of Christian values and virtues. It is a little pond in which (at least, so it appears to this outsider) there is room to become a bigger fish—one who might do something to change all of this. But I fear sometimes that this moral coating is just a thin candy shell. Even in lower Alabama, the influence of the other L.A. is coming. The influence of the media, its double hearts beating in Hollywood on the left coast and Manhattan on the right, has pumped its messages of "only celebrity matters" and "do what you want" into the back roads and bayous and bean fields. And in the L.A. where I grew up—that Nineveh full of people who in the words of Jonah "do not know their right hand from their left"—I felt like a very small fish indeed. A guppy. I was overwhelmed by all I saw. Somehow, that feeling still gnaws at me today. How can I make a difference? How can you?

I visualize those disciples of Christ, sitting in the upper room on that blackest of Saturdays. Jesus is in the grave. They look at one another wordlessly. "What do we do now?" their haunted eyes ask one another. Then Jesus came back. Resurrection! That's the message they were given to share! They had the solution, the answer to life's dilemma of the finality of death! The Good News was gospel! Oh, how I would like to have been there.

Thomas wasn't in the upper room. And being a practical man with a pessimistic nature, he doubted. I'm so glad Thomas's story is in Scripture. It's a kind of verification of the reality of Christ's return. Thomas was brave enough, certainly, to face the world. After all, when Jesus set his face to go toward Jerusalem in John 11:16, and the other disciples quaked at the prospect of almost certain death, Thomas said, "Let's go, that we may die with him." But in John 20:25, Thomas was being asked to do something harder than die. He was being asked to *believe*. He couldn't. Not just by faith. So Jesus gave Thomas what he needed—sight, sound, and sensation. In the face of this demonstrated reality, Thomas crumpled to his knees before the risen Lord. And I think to myself, if "Show Me" Thomas believed, then surely that verifies that it all happened.

Then Jesus said something that has resonated through the millennia since: "Blessed are they who did not see, and yet believed." That's us—you and me. We are believers. And we have been given this same Good News to share! So why don't we? Why do we so often feel powerless?

"I do feel powerless, Lord," I say.

"Why?" His voice is not surprised.

"I . . . just do. Look around at the enormous odds we face. We Christians are overwhelmed on every side!"

"And when has that ever *not* been the case?" he asks. "Those disciples—Thomas included—had all seen the truth with their own eyes, yet they felt just as powerless. And the empire they faced was every bit as overwhelming as the one you face. And I told them to—"

"Wait," I respond, "until they received power from on high."

"My power."

"Yes," I acknowledge. "The Holy Spirit."

"And when my Spirit came?"

151

"They turned the world upside down," I respond. You see, I know all the right answers. I have ever since I was a kid in Sunday school. I just haven't always *lived* them.

"Or right side up, depending on your perspective," God says.

"Right . . . ," I answer hesitantly. For the world isn't right side up now, is it?

"And why is that?" God asks.

"Uh . . ." I don't answer this, because I have no answer. I had a student ask me in class once, "Why—after all God had done in Christ Jesus, after the marvelous spread of the faith in the first three centuries, after the majority of the Roman world (we think) became Christians by the year AD 300—why didn't it continue to spread?"

Actually, it did—throughout Europe over the course of the following ten centuries, then eventually across the world during the European colonization of the planet. At the end of the 1800s, the Christian faith appeared to be an unstoppable force in the world, and European Christians regarded its eventual conquest of all the world with a triumphant attitude of expectancy. Yet here we are, part of a generation that is looking for God in all the wrong places. Our culture regards the Christian faith as but one of *many* on the menu. The missionary task—even in our own once "Christian" land, even in lower Alabama—is as enormous as ever. And we are working with an additional handicap. In a culture that places a premium on "new and improved!" the Christian faith seems old and unimproved. Oh, not to me, but to many of those I meet. They tend to think the faith needs a market makeover—better public relations. Perhaps *then* they will take a new look at it.

"How are we going to reach this world with your Good News?" I ask.

"Oh, I think your real question is a little more personal, isn't it?" God asks, cutting—as he always does when we listen—to the heart of the issue.

"Well, yes."

"And that question is?"

"How do *I* do what you want *me* to do?"

"Better," God answers. "You can talk all day about 'strategies for reaching the world' and yet do nothing to achieve the goal. My people do that every day in churches, seminaries, and conferences around the globe, but you can talk about it only so long before you founder under the overwhelming odds. The bottom line on the early church was simple: my Spirit made the difference. I changed the world. And I still will—through my chosen vessel."

"The church," I nod.

"Only as long as you interpret that not as an institution—as the world does—but as the corporate form of my people. Individuals empowered by *my* Spirit. Which brings us back again to your personal question—"

"How do *I* do what you want *me* to do?"

"Not in your own power, you may be certain of that."

I am powerless in the face of the faithlessness of this age. But the Scripture tells us that it is "not by might, nor by power, but by my Spirit, says the LORD."

"'Wait in Jerusalem until you are clothed with power from on high,' those disciples heard me say. And when I came in Spirit, they were transformed. Empowered. Literally *inspired*. Dynamized."

The Greek word for power is *dynamis*, from which we get our word *dynamite*. The Holy Spirit's power is explosive in nature. So why is the church so often more like a firecracker, going off with a loud bang but moving nothing?

"Why are *you*?" God asks me, more pointedly.

"I need to talk to you about the Holy Spirit," I say in my heart.

God responds, "Here I am—that Spirit within you, listening to you, talking to you—interceding for you."

"But there's so much confusion among your children about this aspect of your nature. When I was growing up and the King James Version was all we had, you were the Holy Ghost—a kind of scary, Halloweenish terminology. And then came the new translations, and a lot of excitement and energy and conversation about your Holy Spirit, within the walls as well as out in the highways and hedges—and not a few arguments as well. And that explosive power seemed to blow apart a lot of churches, and it still does sometimes. The Holy Spirit has become one more thing that Christians fight about. I'm just me, but I know I speak for many when I ask, 'Who are you, Lord, when in Holy Spirit form?' And how do I know when it's you talking to me?"

"The second question is the more problematic, isn't it?" God responds. "Because you *do* know me. I am the one who came into you when you were a child, when you first made me your Savior, and I've been with you ever since as you've struggled within yourself to make me truly Lord."

"Some people think you come and go," I mutter.

"A kind of divine commuter," God responds, and is he smiling? "No. You know my promise: I am with you always, even to the end of the age."

"Then why don't I *feel* you always?" Yeah, a lot of people ask that one.

"Then why don't you answer it?" God says back. You see, he knows that I already know why.

"Because, " I confess, "I don't always seek you."

"Which grieves me," God tells me sadly, and I recall the verse "Grieve not the Holy Spirit." "You know this already," he continues. "You *know* how to block me off from your thoughts, how to ignore my instructions, how to frustrate my intentions for your life. Doesn't that also answer the question about why those wonderful changes in the world seemed to falter around three hundred years after my incarnation? It's clear evidence, isn't it, that you are not the only believer who knows how to grieve me."

"Not by a long shot," I mutter. I'm thinking of countless Christian brothers and sisters I've watched falter along the way—through rebellion, through pride, through judgment of others—

"And now you are judging others yourself," God reminds me. "Instead of focusing on all those *others* who have ignored me, let's just keep the spotlight focused on you for now, shall we?"

I swallow. "Uh . . . right. Okay, all of this is true. I *do* know how to 'wall you off,' Lord—to 'compartmentalize' my mind, as the psychiatrists call it."

"Your 'sin nature,' as my Book would call it. The simple truth is that you do know I am here, that I am available to speak to you whenever you open your heart to me in honesty, to listen and to learn. But that second question—"

"How do I know it's you—"

155

"—is more troublesome. Because the adversary can disguise himself even as an angel of light and mislead my people."

"I . . . I think that's happened to me before . . . ," I mumble.

"I *know* it's happened to you before."

"Then how do I tell?"

"First," the Lord instructs me, "remember who I am in this form—the Comforter. I am come that you might have abundant life—a life worth living."

"So when I hear a voice in my head saying that I have no value—"

"That's not me."

"—that I am condemned—"

"That's not me."

"—that I am unloved and in fact unworthy of *being* loved—"

"That's not me."

"A voice that makes me afraid of you—"

"That isn't me. Don't you remember what my Book says in 1 John 4:18?"

"Yes," I respond. "It says, 'There is no fear in love; but perfect love casts out fear, because fear involves punishment, and the one who fears is not perfected in love.' But what about when I feel convicted of my sin?"

"Then the accuser has a ready opportunity to tempt you to condemn yourself and further compound your sin. True conviction brings a simple choice: resist me and sink further into guilt or hardening of your heart, or confess your sin and experience my forgiveness for it! Only the evil one wants to keep you in that state, holding you in bondage either to the sin itself or to its guilt and shame."

"But," I interject, "that's kind of a narrow line, isn't it? A moment when my heart's ear is hearing competing voices—"

"Then be sure to listen to the one that reflects my Book. I do not contradict myself, you know. My Word is eternal, and my Spirit and my Word will always agree. You should find comfort in that! Not only do you have my presence within you, but you have my Word written down there in black and white to study whenever you need clarity!"

"I know some people who only believe it if it's 'written in the red—'"

"But *you* know that *every* word is true, not just those printed in red letters."

"So . . . your Spirit will always bring the comfort of love—the conviction that leads to confession and forgiveness—and will always be in agreement with your Word."

"And concerning what's printed 'in the red,' know that my Spirit will always point you to Christ. I am revealed to you in Christ Jesus. That was the point of my coming in human form, so that you—like Thomas—can see me. If, like Peter, you take your eyes off me in Christ form, you'll sink between the waves of the storm. The seeming ocean that is this intimidating world will swallow you. Your worship, your praise, your focused attention—all these my Spirit will direct you to give to Christ Jesus. That is where I point."

"It's almost as if you're talking about a different person—"

"And this is the mystery of the Trinity. You know good and well no seminary professor can explain it adequately. You can sit around and debate the doctrine if you want.

Just remember that my Word says, 'That at the name of Jesus every knee will bow, of those who are in heaven and on earth and under the earth, and that every tongue will confess that Jesus Christ is Lord, to the glory of God the Father.'"

"That should sort of keep us from letting the word *God* get all fuzzy, shouldn't it? To keep us *specific* when we talk about you—that we are talking about God who is in Christ Jesus?"

"There is no other name in heaven and earth through which you—or anyone else—can be saved."

"Which is what we need to tell the world."

"What *you* need to tell the world! Don't you get all fuzzy yourself with that 'we' stuff. If my Spirit is truly in your reader, he or she will be hearing my voice, applying it to himself or herself."

I reflect on all of this. Gradually I pull back to my original thought that began this conversation: "How can *I* make a difference in this world?"

"Whom do you think prompted you to ask this question? Or is prompting your reader to read these lines? You *can't* make a difference! I, on the other hand, *can.* *Through* you, as I did through those shocked and shivering disciples when the whirlwind of my Spirit filled the upper room and blew through each one of them. I will empower you—and not with a firecracker either. You are not alone, for I am with you—remember?"

I do. And I am comforted by the abiding presence of the Comforter, the whirlwind within.

Now, we can argue about words and names—and believe me, as a professor for twenty-five years, I've heard plenty of such arguments. I recall one dear friend fulmi-

nating in the hallway in heavy theological language about
the name of God used in chapel in a colleague's prayer.
I hadn't noticed, since I'd been thinking about *what* he
was praying for at the time—God's empowerment that
we might be more effective witnesses. I believe that talking *about* God should never be an end in itself. Talking
about God among Christians ought to always lead to our
talking about God to those who don't know him. In that,
I think I'm about as practical as Thomas. The trouble is,
confusion about the nature of the Holy Spirit within us
has led to confusion about how to do the above and to
debate to debacle—the church at war with the church.
Whenever that happens, you can almost hear the demons
snickering. We've probably spent too much time talking
about the Holy Spirit to one another and not enough time
letting the Holy Spirit speak *through* us to the world. We
need to know enough about this Wind (that's what *spirit*
means in Greek) that is within us to be able to let the
Spirit blow us in the right direction. That direction will
always square with Scripture, so if we are ever in doubt
about the voice speaking to us, the Bible is the measuring
stick. If the Scripture doesn't say God says this, don't go
there! There have been some people—who sound very
Christian when you first hear them—who have provided
their followers with a "new" revelation, that is, something that doesn't match what the Bible says. Whenever
that has happened, churches have been torn apart, lives
have been misspent, and spiritual tragedy has resulted.
This is really the basic definition of a cult—some "new"
revelation of Christ. Paul said this would happen. And
he was so strongly opposed to any "new revelation" that
he said in Galatians, "But even if we, or an angel from
heaven, should preach to you a gospel contrary to what

we have preached to you, he is to be accursed! As we have said before, so I say again now, if any man is preaching to you a gospel contrary to what you received, he is to be accursed!" (Gal. 1:8–9). Now, Paul didn't run around cursing people right and left. He was terrified that people would come in after him and pervert the message he had preached. And they have. We need to give precedence to Scripture in all matters concerning the Holy Spirit. But we also need to *hear* that Spirit within us when God speaks to us—to hear him and to obey.

The bottom line is this: God has placed the Holy Spirit within those of us who know Christ Jesus as Lord. He comes when we accept Christ into our hearts—not at some later "to be arranged" date. Scripture says that the Holy Spirit is within us to bear witness to us of the truth—that is, to help us make a distinction between when God is speaking to us and when that satanic "angel of light" might be trying to mislead us. The Holy Spirit will not lead us any differently than Scripture and will not lead us away from the Scripture, or add anything to Scripture. This is a primary reason why it is so important for us to *know* Scripture ourselves, and not merely be dependent on what others tell us!

Fixed on that principle—based on the text of God's Word—we are free to let the whirlwind within blow us to greater and greater heights of awareness in Christ Jesus. What an adventure!

Model and Qualifier

We are blessed with the presence of the *whirlwind within* us. The Holy Spirit has come to indwell our hearts and minds, to bear witness to the truth of the Gospel as recorded in Scripture and as testified to by other Christians. Scripture refers to this as the "seal" of God—the imprint of God's presence upon us. Really, the model and qualifier that might be of most use here is the name given to this Spirit in the Bible itself—the Holy Spirit. We understand spirit in human terms. It is the holiness of this Spirit of God that we recognize when he indwells us. Our purpose, then, is to listen to that voice—and obey it.

Think About

- "Do not cast me away from Your presence and do not take Your Holy Spirit from me" (Ps. 51:11).
- "Then he said to me, 'This is the word of the LORD to Zerubbabel saying, "Not by might nor by power, but by My Spirit," says the LORD of hosts'" (Zech. 4:6).
- "And behold, I am sending forth the promise of My Father upon you; but you are to stay in the city until you are clothed with power from on high" (Luke 24:49).
- "I will ask the Father, and He will give you another Helper, that He may be with you forever; that is the Spirit of truth, whom the world cannot receive, because it does not see Him or know Him, but you know Him because He abides with you and will be in you" (John 14:16–17).
- "But you will receive power when the Holy Spirit has come upon you; and you shall be My witnesses both in Jerusalem, and in all Judea and Samaria, and even to the remotest part of the earth" (Acts 1:8).

Stretch Your Thinking

Do not grieve the Holy Spirit of God, by whom you were sealed for the day of redemption.

Ephesians 4:30

Do not quench the Spirit.

1 Thessalonians 5:19

Discussion Questions

1. The coming of the Holy Spirit in the New Testament marks the true beginning of the work of the church. Where was the Holy Spirit during the Old Testament? Were there times when the Spirit of the Lord "came upon" some of God's children? How, and with what result?
2. Look carefully at the two "stretching Scriptures" listed above. Do you think there is a difference between "grieving" the Holy Spirit and "quenching" the Holy Spirit? If so, what do you think it might be? Are you aware of ever grieving or quenching the Holy Spirit in your own life?
3. Much debate has occurred in churches in the last century regarding how "the baptism of the Holy Spirit" actually comes. If you want to know more, take this challenge: Read the book of Acts with a pen and notebook. Enter every time the Scripture talks of the coming of the Holy Spirit and what happened. Tongues? Laying on of hands? Water baptism before? Water baptism after? You may be surprised to see the variety of ways the Holy Spirit appears.

4. Many cultures talk—and worry—a lot about "spirit possession," especially being demon possessed. If you are a Christian, do you feel "possessed" by the Holy Spirit? Why or why not? What does that concept imply to you, and what are the manifestations of the Holy Spirit in your own life?

11

"WHAT DO I GET FOR ALL MY HARD WORK?"

I have a pretty simple question tonight, God," I say at the end of a long day.

"I have some for you too," God replies, and I cringe in anticipation of them, "but you go ahead first."

"No, maybe you'd better start," I sigh.

"Do you think you know already what I am going to say?" he asks.

I think about that. "No . . . not really," I respond. "It's just—"

"Then why are you sighing so heavily?"

"Oh. Was I?" I sigh again.

"Are you listening to yourself? Because I am. And your sighs carry the weight of the world in them—burdens I thought I had already disposed of for you."

"Yeah. Well, okay. It's like this, Lord. Every night when I get ready to go to bed, the same emotional pressure crushes down on me—so heavily that I sometimes can't get my breath—"

"Or take the time to talk to me."

"Well, that too."

"And that weight is?"

"That . . . that I haven't done enough."

I pause.

"Did you hear me?" I ask.

"I always hear you. I was just waiting for you to elaborate."

"Oh. Well, that's it, really. I just . . . always feel I haven't done enough. That there are so many things I should have done with this day that I didn't do and so many things I want to do with tomorrow but probably won't. Maybe it's just that I'm getting old."

"If you want to believe that," God says softly, but something in his tone suggests I'd be lying to myself.

"Or maybe I'm just lazy." I sigh.

"Why don't you get back to your first question—the one that undergirds all these feelings."

"All right. God—do you appreciate what I do? Not my sin, of course," I add hastily. "I know that's wrong, and I've repented and we've—"

"Let's set that aside for the moment and stay with this, shall we?" the Lord says comfortingly. So I wheel my thoughts back to the burden—to the weight.

"I mean," I begin again, feeling the sorrow and failure and frustration and anger surfacing in me that I often struggle so desperately to hide from myself. "Lord, I don't want to feel these things, but . . . but I wonder sometimes. You see, I serve you. Daily. Or try to. I try to do what you want, to seek you myself and share you with others and strengthen your people. But—"

"Go on," he says, and I can tell he's not the slightest bit offended, so I feel free to do just that.

"Why do I feel so . . . behind? Why can't I lie down and go to sleep without thinking to myself, 'You did nothing significant today'? When is it—enough?"

God is silent. He says at last, "I'm waiting to see if you'll answer yourself."

"You mean, will I push the question deeper until I suddenly come to a new depth of understanding?"

"No," he answers quickly. "We will hope that happens, of course. I just wondered if you were going to answer your own question—like you so often do; with some cliché borrowed from a sermon, or a movie, or some speech you heard a coach make about 'When the going gets tough, the tough get going.'"

"I do that?" I ask.

"All the time. And quite honestly, you don't often talk to me about it at all; you just talk to yourself, give yourself an inspirational pep talk, abuse yourself a little about being lazy or being a failure, and then you get busy again."

"And I don't talk to you about it?"

"Rarely," God says. Just that. Then he waits for me to talk again.

"Um—"

"Yes?"

"Well, what can I say? I mean, of course, you're always right, and I *do* talk to myself like you said and do the pep-talk thing. But—"

"But what?"

"What can I do about it?" I ask earnestly. "Lord, this really does weigh me down—everything I have to *do* does! And it's all good stuff, and I want to do it all—"

"May I interrupt?"

I smile. "You're the Almighty here. Jump right in!"

"Are you sure it's 'all good stuff'—all these things you want to do?"

"Oh. That," I nod. "Yeah, I know, I need to do a better job of setting priorities and learning how to say no—"

"Could you listen to me for a minute? Because you did ask . . ."

I try to just be still and know that he is God and hear his voice.

"First let me be certain that you know that *I* know what your question is. You've asked if I appreciate all the things you do for me. And of course there would be some Christians overhearing you who would immediately jump on you for even thinking such a thing. 'Whatever we do for God, God does through us,' and so on. Or the variation, 'If you're doing it, not God, then it's not worth doing anyway'—" God interrupts himself and mutters, "I hear a *lot* of preaching, you see."

I nod, for so do I, and a lot of it just makes me feel bad about myself.

"Have you ever preached that way?" the Lord asks me—not accusingly, just as a question—and I have to wonder if there aren't times when I too heap abuse on the brethren for their failure to be faithful—and feel holier than others as I do it.

"I don't want to, if I do," I murmur. I remind myself to review this book to ensure that I'm not doing any of that here. Because, you see, it's difficult at times, this Christian life. And sometimes I know that I'm doing just about the best I can and that others around me are struggling just as I am, all of us earnestly seeking that "Well done, good and faithful servant."

"*Is* that what you're looking for?" the Lord interrupts my reverie. "Is that what this is all about? Simply to hear my 'Well done'?"

"Um . . . some of it is," I murmur.

"Only some?" God asks, and this is embarrassing, because my answer has to be . . .

"Yeah. Only some."

"So what's the rest of all this 'Christian service' about—if it's not really directed at me?"

I'm trying to be honest with myself here. "Oh, I guess there's the professional thing . . ."

"You mean the fact that you get paid for ministry?"

"Yeah. That's an important issue—to me, at least, and to others who are in the ministry. And it becomes an important issue, at times, to those who aren't in the ministry and who think ministers only work one hour a week. When you're in the paid ministry, doesn't that make you a 'professional Christian'? Somebody who has to 'be Christian' as a job? What about your days off, then? Do you stop 'being Christian' in order to take a rest day? Or is a rest day even possible? Permissible? *Forgivable,* even?"

"Wait, wait," God stops me. "Too many questions there, and most of them tracking back to this idea that if you serve me, resting is a sin. Are you thinking that? Because that certainly conflicts with my own work practices—and what I've prescribed for you as well. But ministers aren't the only people who feel that way. Plenty of laypeople have the same concerns, the same burdens, the same sense of self-judgment. I think your question is deeper and wider than that. Aren't you really wondering what you're going to get for your hard work? What *reward* there is in all of this?"

I wince. "That sounds so mercenary."

"It sounds so human, to me. It sounds like a disciple—like Peter, and the rest of them."

I know now where this is going. "You're going to remind me about the problem of comparison again, aren't you?"

"I thought it might help."

Yeah. Comparison. That terrible internal razor of fairness that first came out with my incensed cry, "Why is my brother's slice of the cake bigger than mine?" Never mind whether it actually was or not. Comparison—that great eroder of our personal sense of worth. The great attacker of our happiness. Comparison—based on what the world has taught us to call "fairness"—is what we use to measure our own lives against those of others and determine that we cannot therefore be all right. It's one of Satan's favorite ways to get Christians down on themselves, and then on God. And it is not based at all on any eternal value or spiritual weight.

Comparison is based, instead, on "rank" and "stuff." So, essentially, is this world's understanding of "rewards." Have you seen the bumper sticker I've often spotted on the back of little red sports cars, usually driven by guys too old to be driving them, that says, "The one who dies with the most toys wins!"? I've often wanted to stop them to ask, "Wins what? What's the prize?" But of course they are just manifesting the world's way of judging: "stuff" is what counts, and the more stuff, the more rank. And over against that worldly measuring stick, so powerfully advertised around us on all sides, it's difficult for the child of God to think in terms of— never mind *practice*—eternal values. We find ourselves comparing.

Jesus watched comparison develop in his disciples. They began to quarrel about who was to be greatest among them, as if that would ultimately be measured by position and things. In Matthew 19, Jesus deals with this worldly way of valuing in no uncertain terms, telling them that a camel would get through a needle's eye more easily than a rich man would get into heaven. They were astonished, the Scripture says, and wondered who *could* be saved (you know, if the "best people" aren't). Jesus said that with God all things are possible—which of course speaks of salvation by grace and not by our individual personal worth.

Then Peter—bless him!—asks the question for all of them: "We've left everything and followed you; what then will there be for us?" This launches Jesus into a wonderful description of heavenly values, which doesn't end at the end of the chapter but goes on into a parable in Matthew 20: First he says that many who are first will be last, and the last first—in other words, the whole human system of valuation is topsy-turvy in the sight of heaven. Then he tells the marvelous parable of the laborers sent to the field throughout the day. It's become one of my favorites.

In the early morning a landowner goes to find harvesters and sends the eager day workers, who've gotten up to catch the worm, into his field to work—after negoti-

WHAT DO I GET FOR ALL MY HARD WORK?"

ating a wage, of course. They go to work quite happily, apparently—as do most of us when we've gotten a new job! The master goes back again later in the morning to send some later risers into the field beside them, saying he will pay them "whatever is right." He goes again two more times as the day goes by and the hot sun traces across the sky; then about an hour before quitting time he goes to send a final group into the field—and basically calls them slackers as he does so! No negotiation of wage takes place at this point. When the day ends, he tells his foreman to call them all together, the last with the first, and pay them all—beginning with the last group.

This is where the story gets interesting. He pays that last slacker group the same thing he agreed that morning to pay the early birds. And they, standing at the end of the line, immediately make a "fairness" assumption. They're going to get more—because that would be fair. Only they don't. They get exactly what the contract called for. And then the labor unrest begins. They grumble. Have you ever grumbled? It seems to me a big chunk of this book is my grumbling. "These last men have worked only one hour, and you have made them equal to us who have borne the burden and scorching heat of the day!" And you know, I see their point. I think I've argued it with God. "Look, Lord, I've spent my life working for you, and these others haven't done anything compared to what I have, and look how you are blessing them financially! It isn't fair!" And it's not.

Of course, I really don't want God's fairness—and neither do you. "Fair" would mean the sentence of death, for that's the wages of sin, and we are all sinners. Lord, preserve me from your fairness! I much prefer your grace! Which is really what this parable is about—that and the fact that our worldly interest in comparison robs us of the joy of God's gift to us. When the master in the parable sends the first group of laborers out, he tells them plainly what they will receive. And God tells us plainly what *we* will receive: salvation, eternal life, eternal joy, heavenly rewards that are beyond our current comprehension, and more abundance and blessing than a long-lost son finally returned home to his father's house. That's what we've been promised! And then we look around. And grumble. Like that older brother, remember, in the story of the lost son. Valuing himself on the basis of comparison with his prodigal brother and feeling somehow mistreated. Jesus says to his disciples, "Don't think that way! I promise you will receive whatever is right!" Whatever is *right* in the Master's eyes, not whatever is *fair* in the world's eyes.

The parable ends with the master saying to the grumblers, "Didn't I give you what I promised? If I want to be generous to others, am I not allowed to be so? Am I not free to extend my grace to whomever?" I believe Jesus expected his disciples then and in all times to understand what this means: Don't compare. Don't live your life judging yourself and your lot as the world judges. Instead, adopt heavenly values. Did Jesus's disciples get the point? That's what I find most interesting about Matthew 20. When you read on from verse 16 into 17, you see that Jesus is trying to prepare these guys for his horrible death and for his resurrection. But we see later that they must not have been listening. Why not? Read verses 20–28 and you might see *why*. This is when the mother of James and John comes to ask Jesus to sit her sons on his right and left hand, and the whole group of disciples falls to arguing about status. I have a visual picture of Jesus shaking his head and hitting it with his palm, wondering,

Will these people never get it? Then he says in verse 25, "Don't evaluate yourselves like the Gentiles do! If you want to be great, be a servant—like me."

Does God appreciate my service to him? What a question. "What am I going to get, Lord?" I'm asking, as Peter did. And God answers, "Whatever is right." Then he promises that "whatever is right" means everything. I'm going to get everything I've ever wanted—and much that I cannot conceive—and this will be in the presence of the rest of his children, as they receive the same abundance of blessings in a glorious reward ceremony in the heavenly courts. And I'm spending my time *grumbling?* What a waste.

"Lift up your eyes and look at the fields, for they are white unto harvest. Pray that the Lord of the harvest will send out more laborers! And since you are already out there," I hear God saying to me, "why don't you get back to work? Sundown is coming."

Model and Qualifier

The model for this chapter has been, frankly, the *boss.* We use the term regularly, and embedded in it is a concept of "bossiness" that most of us find distasteful, especially if applied to us! But its basic meaning is superior, supervisor—the owner. All of that God certainly is, especially for those who serve him full time. But the eternal qualifier needs to be *benevolent*—he is the *benevolent boss.* And the word *benevolent* needs some explaining for us to appreciate its value. It means "giver of blessings." Our God is a compassionate, generous, abundant giver, sensitive to our needs and responsive to our requests. He is a boss like no other in that regard—no less our boss for that, but certainly far more than we expect or deserve. He's the kind of boss we simply want to do our best to please, because of our mutual love. It makes this world a great place to work!

Think About

- "Those who sow in tears shall reap with joyful shouting. He who goes to and fro weeping, carrying his bag of seed, shall indeed come again with a shout of joy, bringing his sheaves with him" (Ps. 126:5–6).
- "But it is not this way among you, but whoever wishes to become great among you shall be your servant; and whoever wishes to be first among you shall be slave of all. For even the Son of Man did not come to be served, but to serve, and to give His life a ransom for many" (Mark 10:43–45).
- "But I do not consider my life of any account as dear to myself, so that I may finish my course and the ministry which I received from the Lord Jesus, to testify solemnly of the gospel of the grace of God" (Acts 20:24).
- Read also 1 Corinthians 3:11–15; 1 Corinthians 15:58; and 2 Timothy 4:5–7.

Stretch Your Thinking

Let us not lose heart in doing good, for in due time we shall reap if we do not grow weary.

Galatians 6:9

Discussion Questions

1. Exactly what do you expect from God as a result of your faithful service to him? Have you ever made a list of things that you *need* from the Lord and things that you *want* from the Lord and then separated them out into wants and needs? If you did that, would you be able to say that God has met your needs? Has God also provided some of your wants?

2. The Bible is full of stories of God's miraculous providence in times of great need—the birds feed Elijah (even as he is running away from his responsibilities!); the widow who is thinking of selling her sons is told to borrow pots into which to pour oil from a tiny jar, and she fills up every pot she borrows; and so many other stories. Is it possible that our financial dependence on God is a kind of "thorn in the flesh" that he uses regularly to demonstrate how his strength is made perfect in our weakness? A way of keeping us dependent on him instead of on our bank accounts?

3. ". . . if we do not grow weary," the "stretching Scripture" above ends. But I've grown weary many times, as have most of my friends. What do you think this really means? Does it mean "if we do not let our weariness overwhelm and defeat us to the point that we don't get back up again and get back to the task?" How would you interpret this verse?

4. My brother lived a short but fruitful life for the kingdom and has been with the Lord for many years. I do remember that he loved the first Star Wars

movie and often played the soundtrack as he drove around visiting the sick. The triumphal "reward ceremony" music at the end of that movie helped him imagine receiving his reward in heaven. What kind of heavenly reception do you expect?

12

"Why Hasn't Jesus Come Back Already?"

"Oh!" I say in disgust. "Come, Lord Jesus!"

"Are you really ready for me to?" he asks quietly.

"Unh!" I grunt, surprised to hear his voice.

"Because that's a whole lot you're asking, you realize."

"Um . . ."

"Think of it. Really consider it. One day I *will* come, and it will all be over. Finished. Done. Are you ready for that *personally*? Are all of the frayed ends of your own life tied up? Have you completed all of those last-minute conversations you've intended to finish? Is everything done you want to get done before the last trumpet sounds and I appear? I just want you to clearly focus on what you're requesting when you ask me to come. Have you got the picture? The ultimate 'closing credits'?"

"Um . . . uh . . ." I struggle to catch my breath, comprehending the breadth of that cataclysmic *conclusion.*

"Understand, my child. I hear this from my children all the time. 'Maranatha!' they say, and I just have to wonder if they are really prepared for what they're asking. Lay aside for a moment whether you're ready for it. Do you think the *world* is really ready for me to come? You realize what you're asking, don't you? An eternal death sentence for all of those who have not yet been gathered into my kingdom. On the day I return in glory, every unsaved person's eternal fate is sealed. What about that missionary out there laboring on the other side of the world, struggling to translate the gospel into a language in which it has never before appeared—do you think *she's* ready for Gabriel's trumpet to sound?"

"Uh, no, probably not," I respond.

"What about closer to home? Aren't there close friends of yours, perhaps even family members, who haven't yet given up serving themselves and turned to follow me? Are you ready to cut them off?"

"Um . . . not really."

"When you ask me to return, you're really saying, 'Lord, slam closed that Lamb's Book of Life and get down here, now!'"

"That's not what I *mean* to say," I counter.

"Then what *do* you mean?" the Lord asks me. "That you're struggling today with some common, minor frustration, and that as a result you're momentarily fed up with life?"

"Yeah . . . probably," I admit.

"Another way of saying, 'Lord, why don't you just kill me?'! I thought we settled that several chapters ago."

"Now, I wouldn't go that far!"

"No? Jonah did."

"Yeah, I remember that Jonah did, Lord."

And I think again of that story—the best missionary story in the Old Testament by far. I feel a great personal identification with Jonah—who is, by the way, the most unlikable character in his book. Jonah is the best of examples of the worst of missionaries—a pretty rotten person in the kindest analysis. Why do I say this, and why in the world do I identify with him?

Jonah was called by God to share God's warning with people Jonah didn't like. Jonah ran away—and got swallowed by a fish in the process. A lot of people get hung up in the fish story—some debating if it actually happened (as if God, who made the universe, is incapable of making a fish so huge it could swallow a man). The point of the story is not the fish God appointed to swallow Jonah in chapter 1. If you're going to focus on a creature in the story, then look at the worm God appointed in chapter 4 to interfere with Jonah's comfort. That, it seems to me, is far closer to the heart of the story and to its meaning for us.

If you don't fully know the story, here's a quick review. After Jonah gets vomited up on the shore after three days in the belly of the fish (I've often wondered if he could ever stand to eat tuna again after that), Jonah is again asked by God to give a warning to Assyria. This time Jonah goes—grudgingly—and after hiking into the center of that "capital city of the world" of the time (you might think of New York), Jonah finally begins to preach. It's not our New Testament message of love and forgiveness;

it's a message of hellfire and damnation. To be honest, it seems as if Jonah actually enjoys delivering that message. Ironically, the people of Nineveh listen to it. They respond. They repent. From the top man down, they turn from their sin, believing God's warning and begging for his forgiveness. And of course, from a New Testament perspective, we know what kind of God our Lord is—loving, forgiving, redeeming. God forgives these repentant people of Nineveh, just as he forgives us.

The thing is, *Jonah* knows God is like that, and he pitches a furious hissy fit when God forgives the Assyrians. "I knew you'd do that, God!" he rages. "That's why I didn't want to come!" Wonderful missionary, huh?

It gets worse. Jonah goes up to a high place to look down on the city, actually hoping that God will change his mind again and go ahead and fry these Assyrians after all. It's the same kind of hatred that would cause James and John to plead with Jesus to call down fire and brimstone on the Samaritans. (That was a long time before John became the "apostle of love.") Now, if you read chapter 4 of Jonah carefully, you may get the impression that God begins to toy with Jonah.

If so, why not? God is trying to teach Jonah something. If it seems as if God is playing with us sometimes, maybe we ought to start looking for the lesson. In Jonah's case, God allows a gourd plant to grow up overnight to give Jonah some shade while this "missionary" watches for Nineveh's destruction! Doesn't sound much like God at all at that point. Jonah should have expected something else was coming! But he was comfortable, you know? And that can lull you into a "gourd mentality." I know I've been guilty of having a gourd mentality in my life from time to time. What's a gourd mentality?

"God, make me comfortable!" (As if that's God's full-time purpose.)

Jonah was certainly comfortable under the gourd, but that was *not* God's purpose for it: God appointed a worm, Scripture says, to eat the gourd, so that it shriveled up and died. This sent Jonah into yet another thunderous tantrum, ending in "God, just kill me!"

"Do you do well to be angry?" God asked Jonah. He sounds like a patient parent trying to talk sense to an out-of-control toddler in the grocery checkout lane. Jonah persisted in squalling, and God made his point: "You grieve over a plant—which you had no control over, which grew up over night and withered over night—and shouldn't I care as much about a city of 120,000 people?"

One morning I woke up *very* uncomfortable. It was four-thirty and suffocatingly hot, for I was in Nigeria. Too hot to sleep, I got up and went to take a shower. There was no running water. That meant, of course, that all the toilets were stopped up as well. Now, I was there as the missionary speaker—scheduled to be inspirational, you know?—and at that moment, I was pulling a Jonah. "Lord, why'd you send me here? Just kill me and put me out of my misery!"

He didn't, obviously. What he did was direct my attention throughout that day to the story—and attitude—of Jonah. And this is what I came to understand from the story. God wants us to view the world as he does—with endless grace and boundless love. We, however, tend to view it as Jonah did—a mess that we wish God would put out of its misery! So God set up that little object lesson for Jonah. If the city of Nineveh was like the gourd, then Jonah was like the worm.

Let's face it. We often have a worm's-eye view of the world. It is a gourd to be consumed. We don't care about it. Then again, we didn't die for it, did we?

Perhaps the best thing I can think of about Jonah is that we have the book in the Bible. There's a cute *Veggie Tales* movie about Jonah that ends with the catchy song "Jonah was a prophet, but he never really got it." Yeah, well . . . except he *did*, didn't he? If he wrote the book that bears his name? And who else could have? Was anyone else in the belly of the fish with him, to hear his hymn of praise to God in chapter 2? I'm convinced Jonah did get it, and that's why he could write such a convicting book.

Interestingly, as I reread this book that Jonah wrote, it seems that Jonah casts himself as the worst character, the most unlikable character. I've felt that way often, as I've considered my sin over against the task God has assigned me. I hope that means that I've gotten it too, that the point is not to demonstrate to others how righteous we've been or how clearly we understand God's leadership, but rather—realizing our failures—to press on toward the mark of the prize of God's "Well done, good and faithful servant!" when he does at last call us home. And not to wish to shorten that time, with its struggles and frustrations, but rather to get in all the harvest that we can for his kingdom—to work, for "night is coming" (John 9:4).

"Come, Lord Jesus?" No, I'm not ready for him to come. Oh, I believe I am *personally*, and there are times these days when I find myself longing for heaven. It's just that so many others in this world are not ready for it at all! My job is preparing young people to tell the message so that some of those who aren't ready will be. I hope, then, the

Lord lingers until those I'm training have an opportunity to gather in their part of that harvest. As for the "signs of the end" that some see around us—well, I've never been one to go in much for trying to spell out exactly how the prophecies of Revelation will work out. One day the Prince of Peace will indeed come in the air, and all shall see his appearance. But he is the patient Prince, thanks be to God. His servants have been expecting his return for two millennia and were already impatient for it when Peter wrote, "Do not let this one fact escape your notice, beloved, that with the Lord one day is as a thousand years, and a thousand years as one day. The Lord is not slow about His promise, as some count slowness, but is patient toward you, not wishing for any to perish but for all to come to repentance" (2 Pet. 3:8–9). When Jesus said in Acts 1:7, "It is not for you to know the times or seasons" (NKJV) for his return, I think he meant that is it not for us to know.

So I really don't expect the self-proclaimed prophets of this age to be any more correct than all those who have proclaimed in previous times that they knew when the Lord was returning. None of them has been right up to now, but the signs have *always* said, in every generation since Christ, that he would return at any time. Just as in the first century, I think we need to listen to those angels of Acts 1:11: "Men of Galilee, why do you stand looking into the sky?" The implication is that Jesus is coming back when he is coming back. Get busy! My father used to say, "If God's people gave half as much time to telling the world about Christ's first coming as they do to talking to one another about his second coming, there'd be a lot more people ready for his second coming when it happens!" I think he was right. I've never yet seen anyone

183

saved by the excellence of someone's exegesis of the book of Revelation. People are saved by the compelling story of Christ's sacrifice for their sins on the cross. We have all the details concerning that story in Scripture, and those aren't "cloudy" whatsoever.

Yes, he's coming back! But I hope not soon. Not while so much of his church is sitting around on their hands as the world goes to hell.

Amen! Come, Lord Jesus! But not, please, until we've reached every last person we can with the gospel.

Model and Qualifier

The model of this chapter has to be that of the conquering prince—the warrior hero returning from victory to the rejoicing shouts of his subjects. One day our own voices will shout that victory with joy as we proclaim the name of Jesus and bow in his presence. But the eternal qualifier in this instance is the word Peter used—*patient.* He is the *patient Prince*, waiting to gather in as many as will come before he closes his Lamb's Book of Life. I would love to be a contributor to seeing more names written there eternally than are written there as I type these lines.

Think About

- "'In My Father's house are many dwelling places; if it were not so, I would have told you; for I go to prepare a place for you. If I go and prepare a place for you, I will come again, and receive you to Myself, that where I am, there you may be also'" (John 14:2–3).

- "He said to them, 'It is not for you to know times or epochs which the Father has fixed by His own authority'" (Acts 1:7).
- "Now as to the times and the epochs, brethren, you have no need of anything to be written to you. For you yourselves know full well that the day of the Lord will come just like a thief in the night" (1 Thess. 5:1–2).
- "The Lord is not slow about His promise, as some count slowness, but is patient toward you, not wishing for any to perish but for all to come to repentance.

  "But the day of the Lord will come like a thief, in which the heavens will pass away with a roar and the elements will be destroyed with intense heat, and the earth and its works will be burned up" (2 Pet. 3:9–10).
- Read also Acts 1:10–11; 1 Thessalonians 4:13–14; and 1 John 3:2.

Stretch Your Thinking

Remember what you have received and heard; and keep it, and repent. Therefore if you do not wake up, I will come like a thief, and you will not know at what hour I will come to you.

Revelation 3:3

Discussion Questions

1. If you are a believer, what message first prompted belief in you; what message was preached or shared

with you when you were saved? Did it have anything to do with the second coming of Christ, or was it rather concerned with his first appearance and the cross?

2. One of the reasons the Pharisees—the most religious people of Jesus's time—rejected him as the Messiah was because he didn't fulfill their interpretation of the Old Testament prophecies, even though the early church could recount clearly just how completely he really did fulfill those prophecies. Should this prophetic failure on the part of the Pharisees serve as any kind of warning to us about being certain of our interpretations of endtime prophecies?

3. Many movies—horror movies, especially—have demonstrated a fascination with Revelation and with the "end of days." Do you consider this healthy? Can this fascination for the endtimes on the part of the secular world be helpful in our witness for Christ? Or might this fascination ultimately prove to be nothing but a distraction?

4. Take a moment privately to consider your contribution to the kingdom of God. Is anyone's name written in the Lamb's Book of Life as the result of your direct witness—someone who will spend eternity in heaven because you took the time to tell them of Jesus? If the Lord were to call you home today, would you expect him to say to you, "Well done, good and faithful servant"? If not, what should you be doing the rest of this day in pursuit of those words from him?

EPILOGUE

During the time of the writing of this book, we've moved. If you've ever done it, you know what that means. What to keep and what to save? Sorting through accumulated junk, digging into dusty corners, and rediscovering lost treasures. I found a box I hadn't touched in eleven years (since the last time we'd moved, actually), and—of course—I fell into it, like Alice down the rabbit hole, dropping headlong into the past. Each object, note, and certificate had a memory attached—memories I could not part with, but memories that also made my heart ache. I found things related to old friends, mostly, with whom I've not corresponded in—forever, it seems. And there was that impulse to stop and hunt them up, to call or to write, but I was moving, and there was too much to do and too little time, so these things went back into the box, and *this* time I'm going to find time later to reestablish contact . . .

Yeah. Good intentions. But after so much time, would they even want to hear from me? These are rusted relationships, worn away by time, distance, disuse. Are old friends still friends? Especially when—through the chaos of personal history and uncontrolled events—the relationships are not merely rusted but broken? And what if that brokenness is—I know—*my* fault? In our replacement-oriented society, it's easier simply to start new relationships than to take the time to repair the old. We are, after all—all of us—on the move. And the box of the past gets moved into a *new* corner of the new dwelling, to become dusty again over time. We leave behind, or are left behind, and something new is being built, and we've been conditioned by our "new and improved" society to seek that out. It's shiny and clean. It's not encumbered with painful memory. The new helps us forget. I guess it's a little like a drug.

And sometimes—all too often—the one left behind is God. The first time I did this was when I went to college. I majored in theater arts and chose the school for its emphasis on Christian drama, but somehow that didn't help me remain close to God. Rehearsals every night, performances on the weekends with parties afterward, and somehow Sunday mornings became sleep-in days. I, who had multiple Sunday school attendance pins stuck somewhere in my drawer back at home, became a no-show. God got lost—or rather I did. And then there was that moment when I missed him, and I remembered what I had lost, and I heard that voice—not God's but a lying whisper of Satan—"You're too far gone. After all this time, why would he want you back now?"

"Because I love you," God answered the evil one's question. And that is still his answer now.

This has been a book of conversations with God—questions I've asked him, grumblings he's answered, heartaches I've confessed, comforts he has given. Along the journey, I have tried to be honest—perhaps too honest. I once heard a preacher describe a popular Christian writer as a "spiritual stripper"—a bit uncharitable, I thought at the time, and rather crass, but maybe somewhat true. I hope I've not been that. Mostly I've just tried to be honest with myself in the writing, because I think it's so hard for us to be honest but so necessary if we are actually going to encounter the Lord in conversation and hear his responses to us. I hope that's been helpful to you as you have read, since that was my purpose for writing.

But if you *have* encountered God again, maybe after missing him for a while, what happens now? I'm sure you've had those moments when you've met someone in the grocery store or the parking lot that you haven't seen in a long time. After you've exchanged those effusive first greetings, and quickly caught up on the family, you know how things just stop? There's a choice to be made in that moment. Do you "bump off"—as in "Gotta run. Great to see you again! Call me, let's have lunch!"—when you both know that you have no intention of doing that at all? Or do you reengage in relationship? That'll cost you, of course. Time, energy, and possibly pain. What will you hear that you don't want to hear of this former friend's frustrations and losses? Worse, what will you have to say that you don't want to reveal? Real life chews on us, after all, leaving scars. Some of those scars we'd rather not share with someone who knows us too well. Easier to tell a stranger, who won't carry the story to others we know.

God waits for us to make the decision to reengage him—daily. Only here, the choice is much more costly. God is not just some former friend. He is part of my family. Facing him again is like meeting with a parent after a long estrangement. Ever look at that word *estrangement*? Doesn't it mean that we've become strangers to one another? And the reengagement is—strange. Things are not as they were, not at all. And in moving back to begin on familiar terms—back to true intimacy—we must cross a no-man's-land, a potential minefield of miserable memory and self-examination. It's frightening. And God still waits.

I first met God as did Samuel—in the temple as a child. I have known his voice all my life. I've left him several times and returned, and each time, returning to God after an estrangement has had a price. It costs, quite honestly, *all* of me. But *starting* toward him is easy. It just begins with a conversation. And he makes it far easier to come back to him than the prodigal can imagine. These have been my conversations with him. Where will your conversations with him take you?

Robert Don Hughes is professor of missions and evangelism at Clear Creek Baptist Bible College in Pineville, Kentucky. He has been teaching in colleges and seminaries for more than thirty years and has published fourteen books. He is the author of *Satan's Whispers* and *Talking to the World in the Days to Come*, as well as eight novels. He and his wife, Gail, are part of a new church plant in Middlesboro, Kentucky, called Gap Fellowship. They live on the side of a mountain in a house that grows more colorful by the day. He can be contacted at rhughes@ccbbc.edu.